Tailored resources for better grades

WJEC GCSE English Literature

Margaret Graham

with Stuart Sage

www.pearsonschools.co.uk

✓ Free online support
✓ Useful weblinks
✓ 24 hour online ordering

0845 630 22 22

Heinemann

Part of Pearson

Heinemann is an imprint of Pearson Education Limited, a company incorporated in England and Wales, having its registered office at Edinburgh Gate, Harlow, Essex, CM20 2JE. Registered company number: 872828

www.pearsonschoolsandfecolleges.co.uk

Heinemann is the registered trademark of Pearson Education Limited

Text © Pearson Education Limited 2010

First published 2010

14 13 12 11 10
10 9 8 7 6 5 4 3 2

British Library Cataloguing in Publication Data
A catalogue record for this book is available from the British Library on request.

ISBN 978 0 435 01434 6

Designed and produced by Kamae Design, Oxford
Original illustrations © Pearson Education Limited 2010
pp 15, 25, 30, 41, 46, 57, 59, 60, 67, 100 illustrated by Rory Walker
p122 illustrated by Kamae Design
Cover design by Wooden Ark Studios, Leeds
Picture research by Zooid Pictures
Cover photo/illustration © Thomas Mangelsen/Minden Pictures/FLPA
Printed in Malaysia, CTP-KHL

Acknowledgements
We would like to thank the schools that were involved in this project for their invaluable help in creating exam answers for this book.

The author and publisher would like to thank the following individuals and organisations for permission to reproduce photographs:

p.6 Press Association Images; p.11 David Grossman/Alamy; pp.12, 14 Losevsky Pavel/Alamy; pp.16, 17 E.O. Hoppè/Corbis UK Ltd.; p.19 Kevin Britland/Alamy; p.21 Corbis; pp.24, 27 Peter Cade/Iconica/Getty Images; p.37 John Foxx Collection/Imagestate; p.39 Inspirestock Inc./Alamy; p.42 SNAP/Rex Features; pp.44, 48 Eudora Welty/Corbis; p.50 Charles Hewitt/Picture Post/Getty Images; p.53 Peter Ziminski/Alamy; p.61 Bert Hardy/Getty Images; p.68 Martin Fowler/Alamy; p.69 Jetta Productions/Lifesize/Getty Images; pp.75, 78 Alfred Eisenstaedt/Time & Life Pictures/Getty Images; p.84 Universal/Everett/Rex Features; pp.86, 87 OJO Images/Rex Features; p.88 Hallmark Ent/Everett/Rex Features; p.95 Chad Ehlers/Alamy; pp.96, 116 Andrew Cribb/iStockphoto; p.99 Peter Hince/Getty Images; pp.105, 106 Bubbles Photolibrary/Alamy; pp.109, 122 SNAP/Rex Features; p.112 NordicImages/Alamy; p.119 Jeff Greenberg/Alamy; pp.123, 129 Nobby Clark/Getty Images; p.127 Alastair Muir/Rex Features; p.133 Tatyana Nyshko/iStockphoto; p.134 Nancy Honey/Getty Images; p.139 Arieliona/Shutterstock.

Every effort has been made to contact copyright holders of material reproduced in this book. Any omissions will be rectified in subsequent printings if notice is given to the publishers.

Poem: "Roller-Skaters" by Grace Nichols from 'Everybody Got a Gift: New and Selected Poems' published by AC Black; poem: "A London Thoroughfare Two AM" by Amy Lowell, reproduced by permission; poem: "First Visit to the Seaside" by Raymond Wilson from 'Nine O'Clock Bell... Poems about school', published by Viking Children's, an imprint of Penguin Books; poem: "In the Can" by Rosie Jackson, reproduced with kind permission of the author, copyright © Rosie Jackson; poem: "Woman Work" from 'Complete Collected Poems' by Maya Angelou, reproduced by permission of Virago, an imprint of Little, Brown Books Group; poem: "I Had Rather Be a Woman" by Daphne Schiller, reprinted with kind permission of the author; poem: "Overheard in County Sligo" from 'Collected Poems' by Gillian Clarke, 1997, reproduced by permission of Carcanet Press Limited; poem: "The Lion Doesn't Sleep Tonight" by C.J. Krieger, reproduced with permission of the author; poem: "A Tiger in the Zoo" by Leslie Norris, reproduced by permission of Meic Stephens; poem: "The Jaguar" by Ted Hughes from 'Collected Poems of Ted Hughes' published by Faber and Faber; extract from: "Of Mice and Men" by John Steinbeck, reproduced by permission of Pearson Education Ltd; extract from: "Heroes" by Robert Cormier (Hamish Hamilton 1998), copyright © Robert Cormier, 1998, reproduced by permission of Penguin Group Ltd; extract from: "Paddy Clarke Ha Ha Ha" by Roddy Doyle, published by Secker & Warburg, reprinted by permission of The Random House Group Ltd; extract from: "Anita and Me" by Meera Syal, reprinted by permission of HarperCollins Publishers Ltd, copyright © 1996 Meera Syal; extract from: "A Christmas Carol" by Charles Dickens; extract from: "Ash on a Young Man's Sleeve" by Dannie Abse, reproduced with kind permission of the author and the Library of Wales; extract from: "Resistance" by Owen Sheers, published by Faber and Faber; extract from: "Hobson's Choice" by Harold Brighouse, published by Heinemann; extract from: "Be My Baby" copyright © 2000, 2005 by Amanda Whittington, reproduced with permission of Nick Hern Books: www.nickhernbooks.co.uk; extract from: "Much Ado About Nothing" by William Shakespeare; extract from: "My Mother Said I Never Should" by Charlotte Keatley; reproduced by permission of Methuen Drama, an imprint of A&C Black Publishers; extract from: "An Inspector Calls" by J. B. Priestley (© J. B. Priestley, 1965) reproduced by permission of PFD (www.pfd.co.uk).

Contents

Introduction for students

This book is designed to help students raise their achievement in WJEC GCSE English Literature. It is tailored to the requirements of the specification to help students improve their grades.

The book is divided into the following sections:

▶ **1 Poetry: Writing about unseen poetry.** This relates to Unit 1B.

▶ **2 Prose: Individual texts in context.** This relates to Unit 1A and Unit 2.

▶ **3 Drama: Contemporary and literary heritage.** This relates to Unit 2.

▶ **Preparing for the exam.**

▶ **Controlled assessment.**

How does this book work?

Each section is divided into parts that cover the assessment criteria and requirements of the specification. Useful features include the following.

▶ 'GradeStudio': Sample student answers at different grades, with comments and tips from a senior examiner on how to move up through the grades and put what you have learnt into practice.

▶ Exam-style questions for practice.

▶ Peer and self-assessment activities.

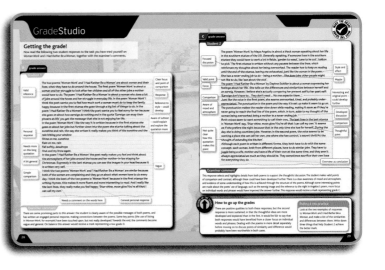

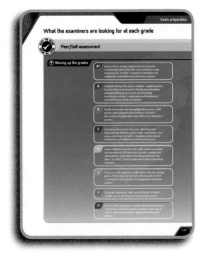

The approach of this book builds on many years of examining experience, workshops, training sessions and revision courses with teachers and students. It can be used with confidence to help you develop and achieve the best grades you can.

We hope you enjoy using this book and find it useful in developing your skills. Good luck in the exams.

Margaret Graham

Stuart H Sage

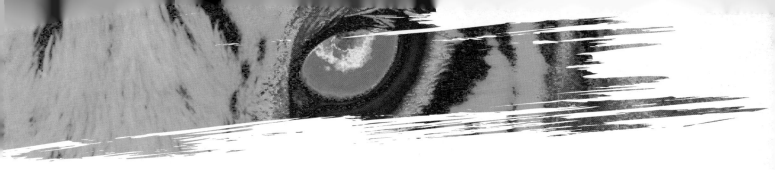

What is in the exams?

You will have to take two exams in order to complete GCSE English Literature.
You will not be permitted to take copies of your set texts with you.
The two exams are as follows:

	Unit 1: Prose (different cultures) and poetry (contemporary)	Unit 2a: Literary heritage drama and contemporary prose OR Unit 2b: Contemporary drama and literary heritage prose
How long is the exam?	2 hours	2 hours
What is in the exam?	Section A requires you to answer two questions about your chosen prose text from a different culture. The first question requires close reading of an extract. The second question offers a choice of tasks relating to the text as a whole. Section B requires you to answer a question comparing two unseen contemporary poems.	This paper requires you to answer two questions on each of your chosen texts (a drama text and a prose text). The first question requires close reading of an extract. The second question offers a choice of tasks relating to the text as a whole.
How will I be assessed?	All exams have what are known as 'assessment criteria', which define what is being tested by the questions.	
What are the assessment criteria?	• Respond to texts critically and imaginatively; select and evaluate relevant textual detail to illustrate and support interpretations. • Explain how language, structure and form contribute to writers' presentation of ideas, themes and settings. • Make comparisons and explain links between texts, evaluating writers' different ways of expressing meaning and achieving effects. • Relate texts to their social, cultural and historical contexts; explain how texts have been influential and significant to self and other readers in different contexts and at different times.	• Respond to texts critically and imaginatively; select and evaluate relevant textual detail to illustrate and support interpretations. • Explain how language, structure and form contribute to writers' presentation of ideas, themes and settings. • Relate texts to their social, cultural and historical contexts; explain how texts have been influential and significant to self and other readers in different contexts and at different times.

What is controlled assessment?

For your GCSE English Literature qualification you will need to complete a written controlled assessment as well as the two exams.

Your controlled assessment will be an assignment linking a Shakespeare play to a range of poetry. For this piece, you will consider thematic links between your chosen texts.

The task will be based on one of the following themes:

▶ Love

▶ Family and parent/child relationships

▶ Youth/age

▶ Power and ambition

▶ Male/female relationships/role of women

▶ Hypocrisy/prejudice

▶ Conflict

▶ Grief.

You may write about any Shakespeare play except *Othello* or *Much Ado About Nothing*, but your poetry choices must be from the WJEC GCSE Poetry Collection.

You may be allowed access to a clean copy of the WJEC Poetry Collection and your Shakespeare text when completing your assignment under controlled assessment conditions.

You will find more information about controlled assessment on pages 138 and 139.

Introduction for teachers

What additional resources are there?

The WJEC GCSE series also includes:

▶ **WJEC Poetry Collection Student Book** supporting every poem in the WJEC Poetry Collection for all abilities and providing specific advice for tackling the Controlled Assessment Task.

▶ **WJEC Poetry Collection Teacher Guide** with full-colour lesson plans and schemes of work, written by David Grant. These lesson plans make use of the BBC footage and other resources in the ActiveTeach CD-ROM as well as providing support for EAL students.

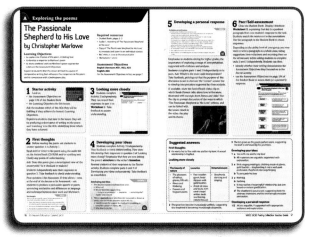

▶ **WJEC Poetry Collection ActiveTeach CD-ROM** an on-screen version of the WJEC Poetry Collection student book together with BBC footage and other resources including grade-improvement interactive activities, handouts and the full Teacher Guide.

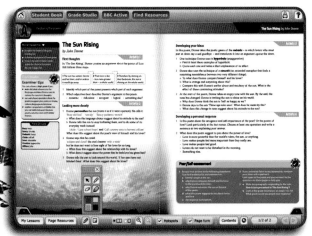

Poetry

Writing about unseen poetry

In Unit 1 of the English Literature examination, you will be required to write about and compare two 'unseen' poems. 'Unseen' means that it's unlikely you will have seen or read the poems on the examination paper before, so you will need to work out your responses to them on your own. But even though it's not likely that you will have read the poems before, you will have seen the question and the bullet points (the bullet points are always printed with the question, in order to provide a framework for your answer), because the questions for both Foundation and Higher tiers are always the same. This is what they look like:

> **Write about both poems and their effect on you. Show how they are similar and how they are different.**
>
> You may write about each poem separately and then compare them, or make comparisons, where appropriate, in your answer as a whole.
>
> You may wish to include some or all of these points:
> - the content of the poems – what they are about
> - the ideas the poets may have wanted us to think about
> - the mood or atmosphere of the poems
> - how they are written – words and phrases you find interesting, the way they are organised, and so on
> - your responses to the poems, including how they are similar and how they are different.

These are the assessment criteria that you will be assessed against.

> ### Assessment Objectives:
>
> **A01** Respond to texts critically and imaginatively; select and evaluate relevant textual detail to illustrate and support interpretations.
>
> **A02** Explain how language, structure and form contribute to writers' presentation of ideas, themes and settings.
>
> **A03** Make comparisons and explain links between texts, evaluating writers' different ways of expressing meaning and achieving effects.

Answering the question

To write a successful exam answer, you will need to bear in mind the following points.

- The part of your answer where you deal with the poem's **content** may be quite brief: a paragraph or two giving the main points about the poems could well be sufficient.
- For the poets' **ideas, or themes**, try asking yourself why the poets wrote the poems.
- For **mood and atmosphere**, it may help to think of the feelings in the poems. Some people find it helps to ask themselves: if the poems were in colour, what colours would they be? Or what type of music would be playing in the background? This will help you to understand the mood and atmosphere.
- When it comes to **looking at language**, you must never just 'spot' a poet's techniques (for example, write something like 'There is a metaphor in the first stanza'). It's fine to use terminology (the labels for language features), but it doesn't earn you any marks – what's most important is that you show you understand the *effects* of the words and phrases used.
- Always support your points with evidence from the text, and explain your ideas fully.

Making a comparison

The poems on the exam paper will have been chosen because they have something in common. For example, they may both be about love, or work, or animals. You may find that the question includes a note of explanation about the main features the poems have in common; if not, it will be because it's very obvious.

The poems will therefore be similar in content or theme (the poets' messages), but because they are written by different poets, they will be different in their points of view, or in the way they are written, so you need to look out for these similarities and differences and write about them in your response.

Getting started: Some handy hints!

A mistake people sometimes make is to treat a poem as a mysterious riddle to be solved. This isn't the case, and the best idea is to start at the most obvious reading.

When you are required to write about a poem you have never seen before, the following hints will help you find your way through.

1   Look at the title. It may well give you an idea of what the poem's about, either through being self-explanatory, or by giving you a clue about the poet's ideas (the theme, or subtext). Either way, it will give you a useful lead.

2   Take time to read and re-read the poem carefully before you start to write – first impressions aren't always completely reliable. To work out the general meaning, a useful tip is to read the poem in sections from punctuation mark to punctuation mark; this really works! You will find the poem sorts itself into units of sense.

3   Often the key message comes right at the end of a poem, so it's important to be thorough, and not to let your attention tail off towards the end.

4   If you don't understand any individual words, take a moment to check whether they are explained with an asterisk (*) at the end of the poem, or if there are any notes to give you a lead. If not, don't worry. The chances are that you'll be able to work out the general meaning from your understanding of the whole poem.

5   As you begin to look more closely at the detail of the poem, underline key words and phrases, and annotate the poem (make notes of your ideas).

6   You may notice the poet has used distinctive imagery (pictures in words). If so, what are the effects?

7   Think about whether there's a specific voice in the poem, and if so, whose? Poets sometimes write as if they are a different character (sometimes called a persona), but they often write in their own voices, too. In either case, what is the effect?

8   Is the poem addressed to someone? If so, who is this? Love poems, for example, sometimes use the second person ('you'), which can make the poem seem very intimate and personal. If the poem is addressed to someone, what is the effect of this?

9   By this time you will be forming an overview, which means you will be deciding on your 'take' on the poem. See if you can sum it up in a sentence or two.

10   Try thinking about what the aim of the poem may be. It may, for example, tell a story, relate an experience, make a protest, or describe a place. If you ask yourself why the poet wrote the poem, it may help you to understand its possible aim.

11   Think about the way the poem is put together, or organised: the length of the lines, any significant pauses, the use of stanzas, any distinctive rhythm or rhyme. However, only comment on these features if you think they help with overall understanding.

12   Finally, don't be shy about giving your personal response. For example, does the poem connect with any of your own experiences, or anything else you've read or seen?

Remember there is no 'right answer' to questions about poetry, and you will get credit for your ideas as long as they are supported by evidence from the poem. It's a good idea to use words such as 'perhaps' and 'maybe' to show that you're aware different interpretations are possible.

You must comment on how the poem is written (its style), but don't worry about using technical terms. You get marks for looking at the words and phrases used, and showing how they contribute to the overall meaning of the poem, not for knowing their technical names. In fact, spotting techniques can get in the way of showing your understanding.

In the exam you are given bullet points (which are always the same) to guide you, based on the hints above. It's sensible to use them, but you don't need to write an equal amount on each one, and you can use them in any order.

The poems will have been chosen so that students will be able to respond to them in an exam, so there's no need to worry that you won't understand them. If you follow these tips, you will understand them!

Responding to an unseen poem

It is unlikely that you will have seen or read the poems on the examination paper before. You will need to read the poems and interpret them independently. What you do in this section will build your skills to help you gain confidence in responding to unseen poems in the exam.

Activity 1 will help you get used to sorting out your ideas about a poem you're reading for the first time. The following steps are based on the framework you will see in the exam.

Activity 1

Working either on your own or with a partner, read and make notes on the poem *Roller-Skaters*. Jot down:
- what you think it is about
- the ideas the poet may have wanted you to think about, and how you know this
- the mood and atmosphere of the poem (remember, this may not be the same all the way through)
- specific words and phrases that highlight, or help you understand, the mood and atmosphere and the poem's possible messages
- anything noteworthy about the way the poem is structured and organised
- your ideas about the poem as a whole.

Roller-Skaters

Flying by
on the winged-wheels
of their heels

Two teenage earthbirds
zig-zagging
down the street

Rising
unfeathered –
in sudden air-leap

Defying law
death and gravity
as they do a wheely

Landing back
in the smooth swoop
of youth

And faces gaping
gawking, impressed
and unimpressed

Only Mother watches – heartbeat in her mouth

Grace Nichols

Did you notice that the title here tells you exactly what the poem is about? Look at the 'Check your answers' box to consider your response.

GradeStudio

Check your answers

- What ideas did you think the poet wanted us to think about – Freedom? Growing up? Fun? Young people separating from their parents? Maybe you think it is about all these things, and more!
- What about words and phrases? Did you notice how many are associated with birds? What is the effect of this, in your opinion?
- What about the reference to 'death and gravity'? How does this fit in, do you think?
- Look at the last few lines of the poem – these are often the most significant in the whole poem, so it's important not to underestimate them. What did you make of these? Why is the last line isolated, in your opinion?
- The lines are very short here, sometimes only one word. Have you included anything about the effect of this?

GradeStudio

Examiner tips

Start from the most obvious reading, and then work deeper into possible additional meanings.

Now that you have written a response to the poem *Roller-Skaters* and checked your answer using the Examiner Tips we can look at some examples of responses written by students to the same question and using the same poem.

The following activity will help you see some of the features of a successful response.

Activity 2

Here are two introductory paragraphs to responses on *Roller-Skaters*. Read them carefully, make a note of the differences between them, and decide which you think is better, and why.

Example 1

> The poet describes the two teenagers as 'two teenage earthbirds'. I found this quote interesting as Nichols is saying that the teens are earthbirds, so it is a metaphor. I think that this is used to show how teenagers are the age group in society who have freedom and are not tied down by adult difficulties such as bills, jobs and marriage.

Example 2

> I think that the poem Roller-Skaters is about two teenagers and how they have no fear, even though the sport is really quite dangerous. Grace Nichols comments on the tricks that the teens complete and the mothers of the teens and how they are affected. I think that the poem may send a message out on youths generally about how they are independent and think they are going to live forever.

GradeStudio

Check your answers

If you chose Example 2 as the better response, you were correct. Here's what makes it better:

- it has a clear focus right from the start
- there is an overview (briefly summing up the main ideas)
- it shows an awareness of subtext in the poem.

In Example 1, on the other hand:

- no context is given – if you didn't know what the poem was about, you wouldn't find out from this answer
- although there is a quotation, this is not put into context and writing 'so it is a metaphor' does not add anything
- the discussion then moves into general, personal response.

Activity 3

In these extracts from responses to *Roller-Skaters*, the students are writing about words and phrases they find effective.

Read the responses carefully, making a note of the differences between them, and decide which you think is better, and why.

Example 1

The phrase 'smooth swoop' has been used to emphasise the 's' sound and make it stand out to the readers. Also at the end of the poem there is a metaphor: 'heartbeat in her mouth'.

The atmosphere of the poem seems very upbeat, lively and has a fast-moving pace.

Example 2

The mood that is created during this poem is a peaceful one, because the poet uses words like 'Flying by' which creates a sense of effortless movement, which is usually quiet. Also by using words like 'winged-wheels' the poet describes the skate as a bird, because it's moving so smoothly. Also Grace Nichols creates a sense of awe in the last verse by using words like 'faces gaping'. This suggests how people are stopped in their tracks in amazement.

GradeStudio

Examiner tips

When you select and highlight detail, show how the selected detail works within the overall meaning of the poem. Remember **PEE**:

Point, **E**vidence, **E**xplanation.

GradeStudio

Check your answers

If you chose Example 2 as the better response, that's the right answer. Here's what makes it better:

- the student has made points, proved them, and discussed them. Can you spot the pattern of point, evidence, and explanation as you read the extract?
- the selected details all fit into the overview (the point about the peaceful mood).

Example 1, on the other hand:

- makes a general point, about the repetition of the 's' sound, without fitting it into the meaning of the poem
- spots the metaphor, without any discussion of its effect.

Annotating poems

In the exam, it makes a real difference if you annotate the poems before you start to write. That means making notes around the edges of the poem as you read it, and underlining key words and phrases.

The following activity will help you learn how to annotate a poem.

Activity 1

1   Look at this example of a student's annotation of a poem, and then how these notes were turned into a written response.

Still going on so late

A <u>London</u> Thoroughfare* Two A.M.

They have watered the street, — *Rain?*
It shines in the glare of lamps,
Cold, white lamps,
And lies
Like a slow-moving river, — *Always moving yet could be slow or fast*
Barred with silver and black.   *City not country*
Cabs go down it,
One,   *Trying to make money – polluting*
And then another,   *Party goers*
Between them I hear the shuffling of feet.
Tramps doze on the window-ledges, — *Poor*
Night walkers pass along the sidewalks. — *No one helps*
The <u>city</u> is squalid and sinister, — *Scary*
With the silver-barred street in the midst,
Slow-moving,
A river leading nowhere.   *Pointless*

Opposite my window,
The moon cuts, — *Likes*
Clear and round,
Through the plum-coloured night. — *Light pollution*
She cannot light the city:
It is too bright.   *Doesn't like*
It has white lamps,   *More light pollution*
And glitters coldly.

I stand in the window and watch the moon. — *From the countryside? Moved to city?*
She is thin and lustreless,
But I love her.
I know the moon,
And this is an alien city.   *Strange — New experience — Why are people like this?*

Amy Lowell   *Very poetic! No rhyming scheme*

* a main road

16

2 As you read the reponse, see if you can pick out where the student has made use of the annotations.

The poem is about a city at 2 am and all the things the poet observes while looking out of her window out to the streets below her. I think the poet would have wanted us to think about how we have polluted our world, as where she is the moon, 'Clear and round,/Through the plum-coloured night' cannot light the city at 2 am because of all the light pollution in the city. I also think she may have wanted us to notice how at even such a late hour the city is still moving and alive.

The atmosphere and mood of the poem is quite gentle yet informative. The poet doesn't use many harsh words. In the last stanza the mood is different, as the poet is showing emotions of love for the moon and describes the city as 'And this is an alien city'. The poem is written very descriptively and poetically. Although the poem has no rhyming scheme it is a very nice poem to read. The poet likes to thoroughly describe the scenery, sounds, colours and emotions to the reader. The poet may like to use her short lines in the long stanzas to create another dimension to the poem, to give its reader the personality of the city.

I found the poem to be exciting. I like the way the poet feels about the city and gives all the characteristics of the city to the poem. The poet is very descriptive, so descriptive that you could imagine seeing the picture she saw when writing the poem. The poet makes you feel sorry for the moon because it is such an amazing thing and lights up dark nights but the light pollution has stopped the moon from lighting up the city and covers all aspects, she even introduces the classes of people into it by having a tramp on the sidewalk and people just walking past him. The people don't care about him, like they don't care about the moon. The moon and the tramp are similar for that reason. The poet describes the road as a river leading nowhere which could mean it's pointless.

A normal night, without pollution, should have a sky of dark blue with bright stars and a bright moon to light up the streets, but this city has a plum-coloured night which the moon can't get past to light the city. The city has this pollution from its white lamps and glitters coldly.

I think the poet is trying to say that the city does not need the moon and that the city should be grateful for nature's beauties such as the moon and not kill the earth with pollution.

GradeStudio

Check your answers

- The student has used the annotations of the poem to work out her thoughts about it, and has reached a valid and clear understanding.
- This is an engaged personal response, and the student has selected and highlighted some details from the poem to support her ideas.
- This response represents a good **C-grade** quality of work.
- Still more focus on individual words and phrases and their effects on the poem's messages, mood and atmosphere, could have moved the student's response to a **B grade** or higher. For example, the use of contrasts, the effects of individual words, the use of words associated with light, colour, and imprisonment, and the effects of these, could all have been commented upon.

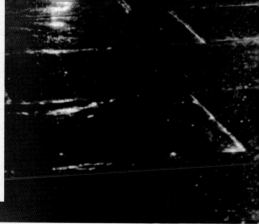

3 How successful is the response?

Activity 2

Make your own notes on the poem *A London Thoroughfare Two A.M.* Be as thorough as possible, and for every word or phrase you select, explain what makes it effective, and how it helps you understand the message, mood or atmosphere. Set out your ideas out in a grid like the one below.

Word/phrase	Comment/response
They have watered...	Sounds mysterious, anonymous. Who are 'they'?
... glare of lamps	Creates a hostile atmosphere

Activity 3

Read the poem *First Visit to the Seaside* and jot down the notes you would make as if you were annotating it.

Then, use your notes to write your response to the poem.

First Visit to the Seaside

I

The new day
Flooded the green bay
In a slow explosion of blue
Sky and silver sand and shimmering sea.
Boots in hand, I paddled the brilliancy
Of rippled wavelets that withdrew,
Sucking my splay grey
Feet in play.

II

It was magic – the brightness of air,
the green bay and wide arc of the sea,
with the rock-pools reflecting my stare
and a maze of wind-sculpted sand-dunes where
slum streets and the Quayside should be.
It was music – not only the sound
of the buskers outside the pub door
and the band on the pier, but the pound-
ing of waves, the loud kids all around,
and gulls screaming shrill on the shore.
It was magic and music and motion –
there were yachts sweeping smooth in the bay
and black steamers white-plumed in mid-ocean;
and ice-cream, candy-floss and commotion
as the Switchback got under way.

III

The spent day
Drained from beach and bay
Green and silver and shimmering blue.
On prom and pier, arcade and b. & b.
The looped lights dimly glowed. And I could see
Stars winking at me, glimmering through
The sky's moth-eaten grey
As if in play.

Raymond Wilson

GradeStudio

Check your answers

Look back on your answer.

- Have you summed up what the poem is about, perhaps using its title as a starting point?
- Have you looked into the ideas the poet may have wanted you to think about?
- Have you discussed mood and atmosphere, using evidence from the poem? Did you think that the mood and atmosphere changed at all? If so, where, and how did you know?
- Have you selected words and phrases from throughout the poem, and explained the impact they have on the poem as a whole?
- Have you discussed the way the poem is put together (its structure)?
- Have you given a strong personal response to the whole poem?

Writing responses to unseen poems

Now that you feel confident in your responses to unseen poems and annotating them for the exam, it's time to build the skills in writing your response to unseen poems.

In the poem *In the Can*, a prisoner talks about life in prison.

Activity 1

Start by reading the poem carefully. As you read it, make notes, then answer the following questions.

1 Sum up the main content of the poem in one or two sentences.
2 Write down the main ideas you think the poet wants you to think about.
3 Make a list of all the images in the poem, and for each word or phrase, explain briefly how it works in highlighting the main ideas.
4 Describe any patterns you can see in the images used.
5 Explain why you think the poet decided to call the poem *In the Can*.

In the Can

Every second is a fishbone that sticks
In the throat. Every hour another slow
Step towards freedom. We're geriatrics
Waiting for release, bribing time to go.
I've given up trying to make anything
Different happen. Mornings: tabloids, page three.
Afternoons: videos or Stephen King,
Answering letters from relatives who bore me.
We're told not to count, but the days mount here
Like thousands of identical stitches
Resentfully sewn into a sampler,*
Or a cricket bat made out of matches.
Nights find me scoring walls like a madman,
Totting up runs: one more day in the can.

Rosie Jackson

* a type of embroidered picture

Activity 2

Now you have the basis for all you need to write about the poem *In the Can*.

Write your response to the poem. Once you have sorted out your ideas, have a go at writing them up, using the type of question you will see on the exam paper:

Write about the poem and its effect on you.

You may wish to include some or all of these points:
- the poem's content – what it is about
- the ideas the poet may have wanted us to think about
- the mood or atmosphere of the poem
- how it is written – words or phrases you find interesting, the way the poem is structured or organised, and so on
- your response to the poem.

GradeStudio

Check your answers

With a partner or on your own, check that you have:
- written about the poem in detail
- discussed its ideas thoughtfully
- selected and highlighted words and phrases, and shown how they contribute to the overall meaning of the poem
- given your personal response to the poem.

GradeStudio

Getting the grade!

Here are two students' responses to the task on page 21. Read the answers, together with the examiner's comments.

the task on page 21

D grade answer

Student 1

Awareness of mood and atmosphere

Perhaps – evidence?

Very simple comments – not convincing

General personal response

> This poem is about a prisoner and his painful and slow life in a prison. The poet may have wanted us to think about the loneliness the prisoner faces, the slow time that passes, the boring routine of every day and the pain the prison faces every day. To show how awful prisons can be. The mood is slow and sad as the prisoner is in pain and has no hope. The poet uses rhyming at the end of lines like 'sticks' and 'geriatrics'. The poet also uses similes, 'Like thousands of identical stitches'. The poet uses a range of punctuation, full stops, commas, colons, to create a more exciting structure and atmosphere. The poet also uses a mixture of short and long sentences to create an exciting atmosphere.
>
> I think the poem is interesting and depicts prison life well, giving the reader a sight into prison life. The poet also uses many techniques to create mood and atmosphere.

General grasp of content and subtext

Awareness of pace

Simple feature-spotting

Empty comments, contradicting earlier points about mood and atmosphere

Empty comment – nothing worth crediting

Examiner comment

This answer starts quite well, showing a clear grasp of the main ideas behind the poem, as well as an awareness of mood and atmosphere, although this is not supported by evidence from the text. But it then falls into simple comments and general spotting of stylistic features, without saying anything about the effects they have. By the end, there is no real sense of the poem at all, and not enough detail has been given about the poem. The quality of this response is of a low grade D.

MOVING UP THE GRADES

How to go up the grades

Student 1 does not write in nearly enough detail about the content of the poem. Tracking through the poem without worrying about general feature-spotting would have shown much more understanding of the poem. Student 2 could perhaps have developed the observations into a more succinct overview, but, overall, this is an assured and analytical response.

Putting it into practice

Look at the two examples of student writing and write down five reasons why Student 2 achieves the better mark.

Now look at your written response to the poem *In the Can*. How does it compare with the work of Student 1 and Student 2? Which level are you closer to, and why?

Write down three things you could do to improve the quality of your response.

Student 2

Clear focus

The poem 'In the Can' is about a prisoner describing to the reader life in prison. Jackson may have wanted the reader to realise how horrible prison is and to think about how the prisoners are turned insane with counting the time and going through the same day-to-day activities over and over with no change.

Overview

The mood of the poem is very dark and dull throughout as a reflection on prison.

Mood and atmosphere fitting into the overview

Close reading of imagery and its effects

In the first line Jackson describes how 'Every second is a fishbone that sticks/In the throat'. This imagery gives the feeling of uncomfortableness, as a bone stuck in your throat would not be particularly comfortable, showing that every second causes pain as they watch it slowly pass. Also the fact that it is a 'fishbone' makes the reader give the title 'In the Can' and 'fishbone' a connective for example like sardines in a can. This relates well with the poem as sardines are squashed and trapped inside a can, as are prisoners inside a jail.

In the next line Jackson comments on 'Every hour' which is the same as 'Every second' making it seem like the prisoners wait for 'every second' to pass and 'every hour' not missing a second or hour.

Astute cross referencing – very closely read

Jackson also says 'slow/Step[s] towards freedom' to make it clear to the reader that these hours and seconds are agonisingly slow. The prisoner also refers to time again as he says 'Waiting for release'. The fact that he has mentioned the concept of time in each line so far emphasises the fact that when you're in jail it is all you can think about.

Subtext

He also mentions 'bribing time to go' showing how desperate the prisoners are for time to go faster. Jackson says 'given up', showing the reader the prisoners are hopeless and have lost the will to try.

Jackson then goes on to say how every day is the same and there is never any change, causing sympathy towards the prisoner. The prisoner then goes on to say 'relatives who bore me' which takes away some sympathy because the prisoner should be grateful but also emphasises how bored they are.

Engaged and well-explained personal response

Extended discussion – clear overview

The prisoner says 'We're told not to count' which relates to the second line from the end where it says 'Nights find me scoring walls like a madman' showing that they are told not to count because it drives them insane as counting does not speed up time. The fact that he is turning into a madman creates sympathy again for the prisoner.

The prisoner describes the days as stitches: 'the days mount here/Like thousands of identical stitches... sewn into a sampler'. This gives the image that there are so many days it becomes overwhelming and they just merge together like stitching in an embroidered picture. This emphasises all the days they have to get through.

Appreciation of imagery and stylistic features

Perhaps

The poem finishes 'one more day in the can'. This picks the mood up as it is optimistic because the prisoner only has one more day. Also 'in the can' relates back to the title bringing the poem in a full circle.

Reference to structure

Personal response for conclusion

The poem is structured in one whole stanza, perhaps to emphasise the fact that your time in prison is not broken up.

Overall I think that Rosie Jackson has captured well the description of a prison and the feelings of a prisoner.

Original and valid idea about structure

Examiner comment

This response owes its success to its close, thoughtful discussion and analysis of the poem. The student has tracked through carefully, selecting and highlighting detail, and fitting this into an overview of the poem. The student arrives at a sensitive and well-supported analysis. This work is of A* quality.

Comparing poems (1)

Now you know what makes a successful response to a single poem, all you have to do is learn how to compare two poems.

It is helpful to use certain types of words to highlight similarities and differences. The following activity will help you to explore these.

Activity 1

Working individually or in a small group, write down as many words as you can think of that can be used to signal comparison and contrast, using a grid like the one below:

Words to compare	Words to contrast
Similarly	Unlike
Also	Whereas

The following activity will help you learn about comparing two poems, by gradually building up to a written response.

Activity 2

Read the following poems, which are from a Foundation tier paper. Then turn to page 26–27 for Activities 3, 4 and 5.

Woman Work

I've got the children to tend
    The clothes to mend
    The floor to mop
    The food to shop
    Then the chicken to fry
    The baby to dry
    I got company to feed
    The garden to weed
    I've got shirts to press
    The tots to dress
    The cane to be cut
    I gotta clean up this hut
    Then see about the sick
    And the cotton to pick.

Shine on me, sunshine
    Rain on me, rain
    Fall softly, dewdrops
    And cool my brow again.

Storm, blow me from here
    With your fiercest wind
    Let me float across the sky
    'Til I can rest again.

Fall gently, snowflakes
    Cover me with white
    Cold icy kisses and
    Let me rest tonight.

Sun, rain, curving sky
    Mountain, oceans, leaf and stone

Star shine, moon glow
    You're all that I can call my own.

Maya Angelou

I Had Rather Be a Woman

I had rather be a woman
Than an earwig
But there's not much in it sometimes.
We both crawl out of bed
But there the likeness ends.
Earwigs don't have to
Feed their children,
Feed the cat,
Feed the rabbits,
Feed the dishwasher.
They don't need
Clean sheets,
Clean clothes,
Clean carpets,
A clean bill of health.
They just rummage about
In chrysanthemums.
No one expects them
To have their
Teetotal, vegetarian
Mothers-in-law
To stay for Christmas,
Or to feel a secret thrill
At the thought of extending the kitchen.
Earwigs can snap their pincers at life
And scurry about being quite irresponsible.
They enjoy an undeserved reputation
Which frightens the boldest child.
Next time I feel hysterical
I'll bite a hole in a dahlia.

Daphne Schiller

Activity 3

In the first poem, *Woman Work*, a black woman speaks about her life in the southern United States. In the second, *I Had Rather Be a Woman*, another woman expresses her feelings about her life.

On your own, or with a partner, starting with *Woman Work*, work through the following points.

- Read the poem carefully, working out its overall meaning (remember to consider the title).
- Decide what you think the main message of the poem may be – what may the poet want you to think about?
- Who is speaking here, in your opinion? What is the effect of this voice being used?
- What is the mood or atmosphere? How does it change at different points in the poem? What makes you realise it is changing?
- Make a note of words and phrases you find interesting or effective, and explain why they have a certain effect on you and how they affect the mood and atmosphere, and/or the poem's messages.
- The structure and organisation of this poem are quite distinctive – can you explain what makes them distinctive, and your opinion about the effect of this?
- What is your response to the poem as a whole?

Now move on to *I Had Rather Be a Woman*, and go through a similar procedure, again working on your own, or with a partner.

- Read the poem carefully (remember the tip about dividing a poem into units of sense if necessary, by reading from punctuation mark to punctuation mark).
- Decide what you think the main message of this poem may be.
- Who is speaking here, in your opinion? What is the effect of the voice?
- What is the mood or atmosphere here, do you think? What is there in the way it is written that may help you understand the mood and atmosphere?
- Make a note of words and phrases you find effective, and explain why they have a certain effect on you. Look at the use of the repetition of the words 'feed' and 'clean', for example; what is the effect of that, do you think? How may it add to the mood and atmosphere or meaning of the whole poem?
- How is the poem structured or organised? For example, the lines are very short; what is the effect of this? What about the fact that it is all one long stanza?
- What is your response to the poem as a whole?

Activity 4

Now that you've read and understood both poems, it's time to think about how they are similar and how they are different. Working on your own, or in a small group, jot down your ideas under the following headings:

	Woman Work	I Had Rather Be a Woman
Content		
Message		
Mood and atmosphere		
Language features		
Structure/organisation		
Response		

Activity 5

Working on your own, try writing about both *Woman Work* and *I Had Rather Be a Woman*. Show how they are similar and how they are different.

You may write about each poem separately and then compare them, or make comparisons, where appropriate, in your answer as a whole.

The following bullet points (which are the same as those you will see in the examination) should provide a useful guide as you write your answer. Remember to consider:

- the content of the poems – what they are about
- the ideas the poets may want us to think about
- the mood or atmosphere of the poems
- how they are written – words and phrases you find interesting, the way they are organised, and so on
- your responses to the poems, including how they are similar and how they are different.

GradeStudio

Examiner tips

In the exam, you will have an hour to answer this question, including reading and thinking time, so it's a good idea to keep an eye on the clock. At first you're bound to take longer. You will be able to work more quickly when you have had practice in answering this type of question.

GradeStudio

Check your answers

Look back on your answer.

- Have you discussed both poems in detail?
- Have you shown that you are thinking about the aims of the poets?
- Have you discussed the different moods and atmospheres?
- Have you selected and highlighted specific details from the poem to support your points?
- Have you discussed clear points of similarity and difference between the poems?
- Have you given a full personal response?

GradeStudio

Getting the grade!

Now read the following two student responses to the task you have tried yourself on *Woman Work* and *I Had Rather Be a Woman*, together with the examiner's comments.

D grade answer

Student 1

Valid inference

The two poems 'Woman Work' and 'I Had Rather Be a Woman' are about women and their lives, what they have to do around the house. The first poem 'Woman Work' is about a woman and her struggle to look after her children and all of the other jobs a mother would have to do. The poem 'I Had Rather Be a Woman' is about a woman who does a lot of jobs around the house and her struggle in everyday life. In the poem 'Woman Work' I think the poet wants you to feel how much work a woman must do to keep the family happy because in the first stanza she goes through a big list of things to do. In the poem 'I Had Rather Be a Woman' I think the poet wants you to feel sorry for her because she goes on about how earwigs do nothing and in the quote 'Earwigs can snap their pincers at life' you get the message that she is not enjoying her life.

Clear focus and point of comparison

Response

Reference to style – could develop

Aware of subtext – could explain and explore the quotation more

Personal response

In the poem 'Woman Work' I like the way it is written because in the first stanza she goes on about her jobs but further down into the poem she starts talking about the sunshine and rain, the way she writes it really makes you think of the sunshine and the rain hitting your window:

Needs more on this long quotation

Shine on me, sunshine

Rain on me, rain

Fall softly, dewdrops

And cool my brow again.

A bit general

In the poem 'I Had Rather Be a Woman' the poet really makes you feel and think about the atmosphere of her jobs around the house and her mother-in-law staying for Christmas. Expressly in the last stanza you can see the images in your head because it is written very well.

Vague

Simple comparison

I think the two poems 'Woman Work' and 'I Had Rather Be a Woman' are similar because both of the women are complaining and they go on about what women have to do every day. I think the best of the two poems is 'Woman Work' because in the first stanza the writing rhymes, this makes it more fluent and more interesting to read. And I really like the last lines, they really make you feel happy: 'Star shine, moon glow/You're all that I can call my own.'

Needs a comment on the words here

General personal response

Examiner comment

There are some promising parts to this answer: the student is clearly aware of the possible messages of both poems, and has written an engaged personal response, making connections between the poems. Some key points (the use of listing in *Woman Work*, for example) have been touched upon, but not really developed. Towards the end, the comments become vague and general. On balance this answer would receive a mark representing a low grade D.

Student 2

Focused discussion

The poem 'Woman Work' by Maya Angelou is about a black woman speaking about her life in the southern states of the US. Generally speaking, if someone lives in the southern states they would have to work a lot in fields, 'garden to weed', 'cane to be cut', 'cotton to pick.' The first stanza is written without any pauses between the lines, which reinforces my thoughts about her being overworked. The reader has to keep on reading until the end of the stanza, leaving one exhausted, just like the woman in the poem.

Style and effect

She has a never-ending job to do – being a mother. She does jobs other people might

Valid point

not like to do, like 'see about the sick'.

Maybe

Focus

The poem 'I Had Rather Be a Woman' by Daphne Schiller is about a woman expressing her feelings about her life. She tells us the differences and similarities between herself and an earwig. However, I believe she's actually comparing her present self to her past self: 'Earwigs don't have to... They don't need ... No one expects them...'.

Interesting and original point – could develop further

Comparison

Just like the voice in the first poem, she seems overworked, tired, and probably under-appreciated. The punctuation in the poem and the way it's set up make it seem to go on.

Aware of mood and atmosphere

The punctuation makes the reader slow down while reading, making it seem as if they're never going to reach the final line of the poem, which, in turn, adds to my thought of the woman being overworked; being a mother is a never-ending job.

Developed discussion

Both voices seem to want something to call their own. The last lines in the last stanza in 'Woman Work' say, 'Star shine, moon glow/You're all that I can call my own.' It seems as if she prefers the night because that is the only time she has for herself. During the

Comparison

Not quite clear how this quotation makes this point

day she is doing countless jobs. However, in the second poem, the voice seems to be wanting a place she can call her own, one where she has control, 'a secret thrill/At the thought of extending the kitchen'.

Thoughtful point

Although each poem is written in different forms, they both have to do with the same concept: each woman, both from different places, have to do similar jobs. They have to juggle being a wife, mother and have a life of their own at the same time, and they aren't always appreciated as much as they should be. They sometimes sacrifice their own lives for everything they do.

Overview as conclusion

Examiner comment

This response selects and highlights details from both poems to support the thoughtful discussion. The student makes valid points of comparison and contrast, although these could have been developed further. There is a clear awareness of mood and atmosphere, and evidence of some understanding of how this is achieved through the structure of the poems. Although some interesting points are made about the poets' use of language, such as the earwig image and the reference to the night in Angelou's poem, more focus on individual words and phrases would have improved the answer further. This response would receive a mark representing grade C.

How to go up the grades

There are positive qualities to both these responses, but the second response is more sustained, in that the thoughtful ideas are more developed and explained than in the first. It would be fair to say that both responses would have benefited from a closer focus on individual words and phrases. Dealing with the poems in more detail separately before moving on to discuss points of similarity and difference would probably have been worthwhile in both cases.

Putting it into practice

Look at the two examples of responses to *Woman Work* and *I Had Rather Be a Woman*, and make a list of the similarities and differences between them. Write down three things that help Student 2 achieve the better mark.

Comparing poems (2)

The following activity will give you further practice in building a poetry comparison, and will help show how different poems can be compared with one another.

Activity 1

1 Look at *Woman Work* in relation to another poem, *Overheard in County Sligo* by Gillian Clarke. In Clarke's poem a woman talks about her life in rural Ireland. For your convenience, they are both given here:

Woman Work

I've got the children to tend
    The clothes to mend
    The floor to mop
    The food to shop
    Then the chicken to fry
    The baby to dry
    I got company to feed
    The garden to weed
    I've got shirts to press
    The tots to dress
    The cane to be cut
    I gotta clean up this hut
    Then see about the sick
    And the cotton to pick.

Shine on me, sunshine
    Rain on me, rain
    Fall softly, dewdrops
    And cool my brow again.

Storm, blow me from here
    With your fiercest wind
    Let me float across the sky
    'Til I can rest again.

Fall gently, snowflakes
    Cover me with white
    Cold icy kisses and
    Let me rest tonight.

Sun, rain, curving sky
    Mountain, oceans, leaf and stone

Star shine, moon glow
    You're all that I can call my own.

Maya Angelou

Overheard in County Sligo

I married a man from County Roscommon
and I live in the back of beyond
with a field of cows and a yard of hens
and six white geese on the pond.

At my door's a square of yellow corn
caught up by its corners and shaken,
and the road runs down through the open gate
and freedom's there for the taking.

I had thought to work on the Abbey* stage
or have my name in a book,
to see my thought on the printed page,
or still the crowd with a look.

But I turn to fold the breakfast cloth
and to polish the lustre and brass,
to order and dust the tumbled rooms
and find my face in the glass.

I ought to feel I'm a happy woman
for I lie in the lap of the land,
and I married a man from County Roscommon
and I live in the back of beyond.

Gillian Clarke

* a famous theatre in Dublin

2 As you work on *Overheard in County Sligo*, either on your own or with a partner, consider the following points.

- Work through the poem from punctuation mark to punctuation mark, in order to divide it into units of sense – do you understand what it's about?
- When you have a general idea of the whole poem, think about its title – what do you think the significance of the title may be?
- Why do you think the first two lines are printed in italics? Remember, there's no 'right answer' to questions like these, so just make a sensible guess, use words such as 'perhaps', 'maybe', or 'I think', and support your answer with evidence from the poem, and you can't go wrong!
- Who is speaking in the poem? What do you find out about this person from your reading of the poem?
- What is the overall message of the poem, do you think? How do you know?
- What do you think about the mood and atmosphere of the poem? Is it the same all the way through? If not, how do you know where it changes?
- Make a note of words and phrases you find interesting and/or effective, and explain how they fit into the overall message and/or mood and atmosphere of the poem.
- How is the poem structured or organised? Have you noticed that the first two lines are the same as the last two? What effect do you think this has? How may this affect your understanding of the poem?

3 Now that you've read and understood both poems, it's time to think about how they are similar and how they are different.

Working on your own, or in a small group, jot down your ideas under the following headings.

	Woman Work	Overheard in County Sligo
Content		
Message		
Mood and atmosphere		
Language features		
Structure/organisation		
Response		

4 Now, working on your own, try writing about both *Woman Work* and *Overheard in County Sligo*. Show how they are similar and how they are different. You may write about each poem separately and then compare them, or make comparisons where appropriate in your answer as a whole.

The following bullet points (which are the same as those you will see in the examination) should provide a useful guide as you write your answer. Remember to consider:

- the content of the poems – what they are about
- the ideas the poets may want us to think about
- the mood or atmosphere of the poems
- how they are written – words and phrases you find interesting, the way they are organised, and so on
- your responses to the poems, including how they are similar and how they are different.

GradeStudio

Examiner tips

- Sometimes the Foundation and Higher papers for the Literature exam will have one of the poems in common.
- You may want to look afresh at *Woman Work*, or you may work from the notes you made earlier.

GradeStudio

Check your answers

Look back on your answer.

- Have you written in detail about both poems?
- Have you avoided making general comments and supported your points with evidence from the poems?
- Have you read between the lines of the poems (looked at the subtext)?
- Have you focused on words and discussed their effectiveness, fitting your comments into your overview of the whole poem?
- Have you shown appreciation of the mood and atmosphere of both poems?
- Have you highlighted points of similarity and difference between the poems?
- Have you given a confident personal response to the poems?

GradeStudio

Getting the grade!

Read the following two student responses to the task you have just tried yourself on *Woman Work* and *Overheard in County Sligo*, together with the examiner's comments. Student 2's response is on pages 34–35.

C grade answer

Student 1

Response to theme

In the first poem, a woman is writing about her life in the southern states of the US. I think the title 'Woman Work' makes it sound like an order, telling her what to do. I think the poet wants you to think about the way black people were discriminated against. The first verse is written as if her life is one big job she has to do. The poem shows all the things she has to do like look after the children. She has got 'The clothes to mend' so she is too poor to buy things. She uses words like 'tots' and 'company' because she has a lot of people to look after. She has to 'see about the sick' so there are even more people to care for. The jobs she does are all lower class and make her sound like a slave. The words at the end of each line are short and snappy, which makes you read the poem faster and makes it more fluent and grips you to make you want to read more to find out about her life. It sounds like she can't breathe.

Valid inference – tone

Inference – perhaps

Tracking through

Subtext

Tone

Probing – engaged

Pace

General response

She writes differently in the next verse. It sounds like she is happier because the sunshine is going to help her. She wants the rain to help her because she says 'cool my brow again' so she is very hot from working and she wants the rain to make her feel better. She wants the wind to be fierce so it will let her 'float across the sky/'Til I can rest again' so she really is very tired, and she wants to be able to rest. The wind is helping her to rest. I think she wants to be left alone and have some peace. She asks the snowflakes to 'Cover me with white/Cold icy kisses'. I think she thinks if she is white she will be better off and people will treat her better. She says she owns nature, but this is impossible. This poem made me feel sad because this lady is not happy.

Subtext

Discussing quite thoughtfully

Valid – probing

Personal response

Inference

Selects – could develop

Straightforward comparison

Inference

The second poem is about a lady who is not very happy with her life, just like the lady in the first poem. She has 'married a man from County Roscommon'. She says she lives 'in the back of beyond' so this tells me she lives in the middle of nowhere. She has lots of animals around her, but not many people. She is writing about being lonely. But she says that 'freedom's there for the taking' so she could leave if she wanted to. She says that she 'had thought to work on the Abbey stage' so she might have wanted to be an actress. She says she could have been a writer. But she is doing normal jobs like folding the table cloth, and she is polishing 'the lustre and brass'. She says she should be 'a happy woman'. This is because she lives in a nice place and she is married. I think she is just very lonely.

Understands setting

Good point – could develop

Conclusion from selected evidence

In 'Woman Work' the woman is very unhappy because she has to work all the time, and she has no time for herself. She is always tired and too hot, and she has no friends. She wants to have a good rest. The other woman has everything, but she is not happy. She lives in the middle of nowhere and is very lonely. This is strange because she is free, but she is trapped by her life. Both women are unhappy, but for different reasons. I like these poems because they tell stories about the lives of two women. I preferred the first poem because the woman had no choice in her life, but she was able to dream to be free.

Insight

Response to comparison

Examiner comment

This is an engaged discussion of both poems. The student has selected and highlighted detail from both poems and has expressed a preference, with reasons, and shown main points of similarity and difference, although these could have been developed. This answer would receive a mark representing a high grade C.

Peer/Self-assessment

Now look at your written response to a comparison of two unseen poems. How does it compare with the work of Student 1 and Student 2 on pages 32–35?

You could carry out the steps below on your own work, or swap with a partner, looking at each other's written responses.

- Annotate the response in the same way as the examiner annotated Student 1 and Student 2's responses.
- Now try to grade the answer, using the mark scheme in 'Moving up the grades' on page 137.
- Write down three things that would improve the quality of the response.
- Looking at your own work, decide which skills you have developed and used successfully in this response.
- Which skills do you need to develop further?
- Plan how you will achieve the improvements that have been identified as appropriate to your own work.

GradeStudio

'Woman Work' by Maya Angelou and 'Overheard in County Sligo' by Gillian Clarke are both poems from the perspective of an oppressed woman. However, the context of their subjugation is very different.

> **Overview**

'Woman Work' is about a black woman experiencing life in the southern sates of the US, an area known for its racism and discrimination. The timing of this poem is unknown, but the tasks listed may suggest that it is either at the time of slavery or soon after it was abolished when black people were seen as the lowest in society. 'Overheard in County Sligo' however is about a woman's life in rural Ireland. Her oppression is because of her life choices. She 'married a man' and lives now 'in the back of beyond'. She feels that she's trapped by normality whereas Angelou's character is trapped by her birth and her skin; she's trapped by the narrow minds around her.

> **Context**

> **Assured overview and comparison**

Both poets write these from a feminist point of view; seeing how women must cope in society, and what their expected positions in the world are. They want us to think about what women do and how expectations affect them. In 'Woman Work' there is almost an atmosphere of desperate release. It is a dramatic monologue focused on her entirely. This is her struggle and her wishes; however by using anonymity the poet has allowed it to become generalisable to all women living through this situation.

> **Style**

> **Interesting point about style**

The rhyme scheme at the start of 'Woman Work' emphasises the sheer amount of work she has to do. It gives it a staccato rhythm that creates a hurried theme, perhaps suggesting the short time she has to complete these tasks. It also makes it almost a routine, this is regular; her normality is all work and no rest. It allows us to understand why then she turns to nature and almost begs for release. She looks to the sun and rain to 'cool [her] brow', to comfort her. Her life has no comfort, nature is the only soothing element in the poem, the only rest from the work listed. Then the wishes become more desperate, she not only wishes for comfort but for death. The extremeness of this shows how truly bad her situation is, 'let me float across the sky/'Til I can rest again', 'Let me rest tonight'. This narrator wishes for heaven and a chance to rest from all her work.

> **Structure and effect**

> **Perhaps – sensitive inference**

The narrator of 'Woman Work' calls to all of nature and creates a poignant ending which outlines her desolate situation. 'You're all that I can call my own'. She has no other possessions, nothing she can say is hers except the nature around her. She looks to nature for all possessions and people that are missing from her life; a caring mother to soothe, 'cool my brow', a lover to be cared for by, 'icy kisses'. She turns to nature for replacements, things that her situation in life has not allowed her.

> **Valid inference**

Sensitive response

'Overheard in County Sligo' suggests more of a narrator enslaved in domesticity. This woman is suppressed not because of her birth or skin but because of her safe choices. She chose to marry and move to the country, she didn't look to put herself ahead or make something of herself. It portrays a woman halfway through her life realising her regrets and suffering from the routine of normality. In contrast to 'Woman Work' all this woman has are nature and possessions, 'a field of cows', but she unlike the narrator in 'Woman Work' finds no comfort in these things.

Confident comparison

Personal response

Although the routine in 'Overheard in County Sligo' isn't as busy as in 'Woman Work' this almost seems crueller. Her small chores aren't fulfilling enough, they don't stop her thinking about the dreams she once had that won't come true. She won't be an actress at the 'Abbey' (a well-known theatre in Dublin), or publish a 'book'. Her feelings show that she already is buried in the country; this woman does not wish for death or release as in 'Woman Work' mainly because she knows that her life isn't bad enough to wish for that. But also this isn't the release she's looking for, she wants excitement, not comfort.

Perhaps

Astute comment

Both poems make me think about the situation of women in history and society nowadays. Although women's situations in history have been monumentally worse, even the humdrum of routine in everyday life can oppress women. The expectations on women throughout time and the oppression they feel because of it is shown in both these poems.

Confident conclusion, pulling both poems together

Examiner comment

This is a well-sustained and assured response to the poems. There is a confident overview and understanding of possible interpretations, and these are supported by aptly selected detail. Discussion of both poems, as well as of connections between them, is well focused and sensitive. This is a clear A* response.

How to go up the grades

Although both responses are engaged and detailed, Student 2 goes into much more depth and closer analysis, as well as developing ideas more.

Putting it into practice

Look at the two responses to *Woman Work* and *Overheard in County Sligo* and make a list of the similarities and differences between them. Write down three reasons why Student 2 achieves the better mark.

The question for both Foundation and Higher tiers is always the same, although the poems you are asked to compare may be different.

Exam question

Write about both poems and their effect on you. Show how they are similar and how they are different.

You may write about each poem separately and then compare them, or make comparisons where appropriate in your answer as a whole.

You may wish to include some or all of these points:

▶ the content of the poems – what they are about

▶ the ideas the poets may have wanted us to think about

▶ the mood or atmosphere of the poems

▶ how they are written – words and phrases you find interesting, the way they are organised, and so on

▶ your responses to the poems, including how they are similar and how they are different.

Foundation tier poems

The Lion Doesn't Sleep Tonight

His eyes
Dulled by years
Of iron bars and cold hard ground
Paces in circles
Looking but never seeing
Past the cage that holds his soul
First one way
Then another
Worn, torn and beaten by time
While those who come to look
And gaze at this king
Say
What a magnificent beast
What a beautiful animal
But all that really remains
Is a coat of skin
And sad shrouded eyes
Pacing day and night
In never ending circles
First one way and then another

C.J. Krieger

A Tiger in the Zoo

He stalks in his vivid stripes
The few steps of his cage,
On pads of velvet quiet,
In his quiet rage.

He should be lurking in shadow,
Sliding through long grass
Near the water hole
Where plump deer pass.

He should be snarling around houses
At the jungle's edge,
Baring his white fangs, his claws,
Terrorising the village!

But he's locked in a concrete cell,
His strength behind bars,
Stalking the length of his cage,
Ignoring visitors.

He hears the last voice at night,
The patrolling cars,
And stares with his brilliant eyes
At the brilliant stars.

Leslie Norris

Higher tier poems

A Tiger in the Zoo

He stalks in his vivid stripes
The few steps of his cage,
On pads of velvet quiet,
In his quiet rage.

He should be lurking in shadow,
Sliding through long grass
Near the water hole
Where plump deer pass.

He should be snarling around houses
At the jungle's edge,
Baring his white fangs, his claws,
Terrorising the village!

But he's locked in a concrete cell,
His strength behind bars,
Stalking the length of his cage,
Ignoring visitors.

He hears the last voice at night,
The patrolling cars,
And stares with his brilliant eyes
At the brilliant stars.

Leslie Norris

The Jaguar

The apes yawn and adore their fleas in the sun.
The parrots shriek as if they were on fire, or strut
Like cheap tarts to attract the stroller with the nut.
Fatigued with indolence, tiger and lion

Lie still as the sun. The boa-constrictor's coil
Is a fossil. Cage after cage seems empty, or
Stinks of sleepers from the breathing straw.
It might be painted on a nursery wall.

But who runs like the rest past these arrives
At a cage where the crowd stands, stares, mesmerized,
As a child at a dream, at a jaguar hurrying enraged
Through prison darkness after the drills of his eyes

On a short fierce fuse. Not in boredom –
The eye satisfied to be blind in fire,
By the bang of blood in the brain deaf the ear –
He spins from the bars, but there's no cage to him

More than to the visionary his cell:
His stride is wildernesses of freedom:
The world rolls under the long thrust of his heel.
Over the cage floor the horizons come.

Ted Hughes

GradeStudio

Examiner tips

Remember, in the exam you will have
one hour to answer the poetry question.

2 Prose

Individual texts in context

You will study and answer questions on **two** prose texts in the examination.

In **Unit 1** you will answer questions on **one** of the following texts from a different culture:

* *Of Mice and Men* by John Steinbeck
* *Anita and Me* by Meera Syal
* *To Kill a Mockingbird* by Harper Lee
* *I Know Why the Caged Bird Sings* by Maya Angelou
* *Chanda's Secrets* by Allan Stratton

In **Unit 2** you will answer questions **either** on **one** of the following contemporary prose texts:

* *Paddy Clarke Ha Ha Ha* by Roddy Doyle
* *Heroes* by Robert Cormier
* *Never Let Me Go* by Kazuo Ishiguro
* *About a Boy* by Nick Hornby
* *Resistance* by Owen Sheers

or on **one** of the following literary heritage prose texts:

* *Silas Marner* by George Eliot
* *Pride and Prejudice* by Jane Austen
* *A Christmas Carol* by Charles Dickens
* *Lord of the Flies* by William Golding
* *Ash on a Young Man's Sleeve* by Dannie Abse

For all these prose texts, the pattern of questions will be the same, for both Foundation and Higher tiers, in both units.

* First, you will answer a single question, basing your response on a close reading of an **extract** from the prose text, which is printed on the exam paper. This should take you about **20 minutes**, including reading time.
* Then you will choose one of two essay titles, where you will show your knowledge of the **whole text**. This should take you about **40 minutes**, including thinking, planning, and checking time.

These are the assessment criteria that you will be assessed against.

Assessment Objectives:

AO1 Respond to texts critically and imaginatively; select and evaluate relevant textual detail to illustrate and support interpretations.

AO2 Explain how language, structure and form contribute to writers' presentation of ideas, themes and settings.

2.1 Prose extract questions

In Unit 1 you will respond to an extract from the 'different cultures' prose text you have studied, and in Unit 2 you will respond to an extract from the other prose text you have studied, either a contemporary prose text or a heritage prose text.

The pattern of questions will be similar for all prose texts in both units. The following questions are typical of the questions you are likely to see in your exams.

Notice that questions tend to focus on either **characters**, or on **mood and atmosphere** (or **thoughts and feelings** on the Foundation tier).

Higher tier questions

On the Higher tier you will find questions such as:

▶ With close reference to the extract, show how … creates mood and atmosphere here.
▶ Look closely at how … speaks and behaves here. How does it affect your feelings towards him/her?
▶ Look closely at how … speaks and behaves here. What does it reveal of his/her state of mind?
▶ Look closely at how … speaks and behaves here. What does it reveal about his/her feelings?
▶ How does … suggest …'s feelings in this extract?
▶ Look closely at how … and … speak and behave here. What does it reveal about their relationship?

Foundation tier questions

On the Foundation tier you will find questions such as:

▶ What do you think of the way … speaks and behaves here? Give reasons for what you say, and remember to support your answer with words and phrases from the text.

▶ What does this extract show you about …'s feelings? Remember to support your answer with words and phrases from the extract.

▶ What does this extract reveal about the relationship between … and …? Give reasons for what you say, and support your answers with words and phrases from the text.

▶ What impressions do you get of … here? Remember to support your answer with words and phrases from the extract.

▶ What are your thoughts and feelings as you read this extract? Write about words and phrases you find effective in creating these thoughts and feelings, and explain why you find them effective.

character

feelings

mood

atmosphere

GradeStudio

MAKE THE GRADE

Examiner tips

In the exam you will improve your answer if you:

● keep a clear focus on the question throughout your response

● select key details from throughout the extract, being as thorough as you can, while making sure everything you select is relevant to the question

● link the points you select and comment on to the overview (your 'take' on the question).

Focusing your response

The following extract from *Of Mice and Men* introduces Curley, one of the main characters in the novel, for the first time. Curley is unpleasant and aggressive, and this is immediately apparent in his attitude to George and Lennie, the central characters in the novel, who have just arrived to take up jobs on the ranch owned by Curley's father.

Read the extract, then look at the activities on the next page.

Activity 1 will help you understand what makes for an effective opening to a character-based extract question.

Activity 2 will help you focus from the very beginning of your response to a prose text.

Of Mice and Men

At that moment a young man came into the bunk house; a thin young man with a brown face, with brown eyes and a head of tightly curled hair. He wore a work glove on his left hand, and, like the boss, he wore high-heeled boots. 'Seen my old man?' he asked.

The swamper said: 'He was here jus' a minute ago, Curley. Went over to the cook-house, I think.'

'I'll try to catch him,' said Curley. His eyes passed over the new men and he stopped. He glanced coldly at George and then at Lennie. His arms gradually bent at the elbows and his hands closed into fists. He stiffened and went into a slight crouch. His glance was at once calculating and pugnacious. Lennie squirmed under the look and shifted his feet nervously. Curley stepped gingerly close to him.

'You the new guys the old man was waitin' for?'

'We just come in,' said George.

'Let the big guy talk.'

Lennie twisted with embarrassment.

George said: 'S'pose he don't want to talk?'

Curley lashed his body around. 'By Christ, he's gotta talk when he's spoke to. What the hell are you gettin' into it for?'

'We travel together,' said George coldly.

'Oh, so it's that way.'

George was tense and motionless. 'Yeah, it's that way.'

Lennie was looking helplessly to George for instruction.

'An' you won't let the big guy talk, is that it?'

'He can talk if he wants to tell you anything.' He nodded slightly to Lennie.

'We jus' come in,' said Lennie softly.

Curley stared levelly at him. 'Well, nex' time you answer when you're spoke to.' He turned towards the door and walked out, and his elbows were still bent out a little.

Activity 1

Read the following openings to responses to this extract from *Of Mice and Men*. The students are writing in response to the question:

With close reference to the extract, show how John Steinbeck presents Curley here.

As you read the responses, consider to what extent the students have focused clearly on the question. In your opinion, which example gives the best overview of the extract?

Example 1

Steinbeck describes Curley as a 'thin young man' with a 'brown face', suggesting his personality, which can be reflected as being immature. In addition to this Curley wears a 'work glove on his left hand', implying that he does have a role in the ranch. Furthermore it shows that Curley is not spoilt in any way because of his status on the ranch...

Example 2

This extract presents the first heated encounter between Lennie and Curley. Curley is a character consumed by violence in order to retain his role of 'alpha-male' and preserve his most prized possessions, first, his respect, and second, his scandalous wife. He represents a corrupted authority. His high-heeled boots may show his anxiety to show his authority, and, perhaps, his insecurity about his height...

Activity 2

1 Choose one of the prose texts you are studying and decide which character you are going to focus on. Select an extract that shows this character speaking and behaving in a significant way. The extract should be fairly short (about a page is ideal). Ask your teacher for help in selecting a suitable extract, if necessary.

2 Choose one of the extract questions on page 47 (Activity 3) to provide the focus of your question.

3 Now write the first few sentences of your response to the question you have created.

MOVING UP THE GRADES

GradeStudio

How to go up the grades

There are positive qualities to both of the responses in Activity 1. Example 1 selects and highlights some apt details, but because the extract has not been set in any clear context, the points made are not really developed or convincing.

Example 2 is better: it starts with a confident overview, includes an evaluation of Curley's character, and provides alternative interpretations of Curley's 'high-heeled boots'.

Putting it into practice

Read the two responses and the comments on them again. Now look at the opening sentences you wrote for the character-based extract you chose from one of your prose set texts. How would you rate what you wrote, comparing it with the levels of response in Examples 1 and 2 above?

Making an effective opening

Read the following extract from *Heroes* by Robert Cormier. The novel is set during the Second World War, in Frenchtown, America, and is told from the point of view of 15-year-old Francis. In this extract he feels that he has let down a girl, Nicole, of whom he was very fond, by not being brave enough to intervene when she was molested by a respected older man, Larry LaSalle.

Heroes

A heat wave gripped Frenchtown, the heat almost visible in the air. People moved as if in a slow-motion movie, gathering on front lawns and piazzas in the evening after the shops closed, hoping for a breeze to cool them off. Men walked slowly as they went off to work in the shops as weary-looking in the morning as they were late in the day, after their shifts were over.

For three days, I haunted Sixth Street at all hours, standing across the street and looking up at the second floor of Nicole's house, venturing sometimes into the yard, hoping that I might catch a glimpse of her coming or going or at a window. Despite the heat, the piazza on Nicole's second floor tenement remained vacant. The windows were open to allow cooler air to enter the tenement but no one came or went.

Nicole's father left the tenement to go to the shop just before seven o'clock in the morning and returned shortly after five in the afternoon and I avoided him, kept away from the street during those times.

A small boy in the house across the street from Nicole's rode his bicycle endlessly on the sidewalk and gazed at me occasionally as I waited. Finally, squinting against the sun, he asked: 'Why are you here all the time?'

I shrugged. 'Waiting.'

'Are you the bogey man?' he asked, scratching his chin.

Yes, I wanted to say. A kind of bogey man who does terrible things like letting his girl get hurt and attacked, purposely avoiding even in my mind that terrible word: what had actually happened to her.

The boy waited a moment for my reply then pedalled back into his yard, silent as he gazed at me over his shoulder. He went into the house and did not come out again.

GradeStudio

Examiner tips

MAKE THE GRADE · MAKE THE GRADE ✔

When writing about mood and atmosphere, you should:

- decide from the outset what the mood and atmosphere is, or what your thoughts and feelings are (sad, tense, angry, and so on)
- be aware that the mood and atmosphere may well not be the same all the way through (just as with poetry), and you can show an awareness of that in your introduction
- provide some sort of context for the extract near the start of your response (that is, show how it fits into the text as a whole), as with character-type extract questions.

Activity 1

Read the following five responses to this extract.

As you read the first three openings, consider to what extent the students have focused on the Higher tier question:

With close reference to the extract, show how Robert Cormier creates mood and atmosphere here.

Example 1

Before this extract Nicole was raped by Larry LaSalle in the Wreck Centre where Francis was watching. He was so shocked that he couldn't do anything. After the incident happened he tried to disguise himself, until Nicole saw him and thought he betrayed her. As Francis said: 'I saw my betrayal in her eyes.' This is why he's sorry and wants her forgiveness because he feels guilty.

The first sentence of the extract begins with 'A heat wave gripped Frenchtown, the heat almost visible in the air.' This implies that there was an unbearable heat surrounding Frenchtown. 'For three days, I haunted Sixth Street at all hours, standing across the street and looking up at the second floor of Nicole's house…'. This suggests to me that he wants to tell Nicole something important, but is too afraid to actually see her because he will probably freeze up and forget. 'Nicole's father left the tenement to go to the shop just before seven o'clock in the morning and returned shortly after five in the afternoon…'. This sentence shows that something is really bothering him, and he needs to speak with Nicole. This is because he has been there, at her house, for a long time, and even knows when her father leaves and returns home. Furthermore I think he's anxious to reveal his thoughts urgently. This makes me feel very sorry for him.

Example 2

Cormier starts with the weather to create a foreboding atmosphere, 'the heat almost visible in the air'. This makes the heat seem very heavy and immediately turns the atmosphere slightly uncomfortable. He also links Frenchtown to a Hollywood theme when the people are described as moving 'as if in a slow-motion movie'. However, the fact that it's slow-motion suggests something is wrong.

Cormier also creates the foreboding mood and atmosphere as relating to what is happening to Francis. He describes the men as 'weary-looking' owing to the heat. These men may always be 'weary-looking', but as this is a recollection from Francis, and these three days were awful to him, everything else appears so, when seen through his eyes.

Furthermore, Cormier describes Francis as haunting when he is hanging around Nicole's house: 'I haunted Sixth Street at all hours'. This word has immediate connotations of death, creating a very morbid mood. Also, it gives the reader the feeling that, after the incident between Nicole and Larry LaSalle, Francis has died inside and is now something of a ghost. The fact that no one else saw him, yet he was constantly there, is similar to a ghost.

Example 3

In this extract from the book 'Heroes', Francis the main character is describing the scene in Frenchtown and the atmosphere. He starts by saying 'A heat wave gripped Frenchtown…' He says this so the reader really feels what Francis feels. Then he goes on to describe how the heat is 'almost visible in the air'. The writer would put this in to make you imagine how hot it is and how unbearable it must be.

In the next part the story goes on to say how Francis is haunting Nicole's house waiting for a sign or a glimpse. He is doing this because before the extract Nicole has been raped by Larry LaSalle and Francis had not done anything to stop this.

When he saw Nicole that night he felt he betrayed her and he wanted to apologise, which brings the story to the extract I am reading now.

Activity 2

As you read the last two openings, consider to what extent the students have focused on the Foundation tier question:

What are your thoughts and feelings as you read this extract? Give reasons for your answer and remember to support it with words and phrases from the extract.

In your opinion, which examples have a clear focus and state their point of view right from the start? Also consider whether the students have provided a context for the extract. Either individually, or in a small group, put the responses, for either the Higher tier, or the Foundation tier, or both, in rank order.

Example 4

My thoughts and feelings on this extract were that I thought Francis was lonely, upset, waiting for 'his girl'. Francis was waiting for her for several hours. The text says, 'I haunted Sixth Street at all hours' and 'Nicole's father left the tenement to go to the shop just before seven o'clock in the morning and returned shortly after five in the afternoon'. I feel sorry for Francis because he was distraught at 'letting his girl get hurt and attacked'. He is in love with her and he let that happen to her, he is waiting there just so that he can see her again, and the text even says 'venturing sometimes into the yard, hoping that I might catch a glimpse of her'.

Example 5

My thoughts and feelings as I read this extract were that I kind of felt sorry for Francis because he loves this girl so much that even just a glimpse of the girl would satisfy but it sounds like he is blaming himself for what happened to the girl. I think Francis hovers round Nicole's place maybe because he feels sorry for leaving her and wants to apologise but it sounds like he is too scared to go to her house and say it. He maybe is too scared in case something bad will happen like Nicole will leave him for ever.

The following activity will help you to see what makes a strong, effective opening for a response to a question on mood and atmosphere/thoughts and feelings.

Activity 3

1 Choose an extract from one of your prose texts in which you think there is evidence of a strong mood and atmosphere, or one that creates strong thoughts and feelings.

2 Choose the focus of your response (mood and atmosphere, which is typically found on the Higher tier, or thoughts and feelings, which is more likely to be found on the Foundation tier).

3 Write the opening of your response to your question:

With close reference to the extract, show how ... creates mood and atmosphere here.

Or

What are your thoughts and feelings as you read this extract?

GradeStudio

How to go up the grades

There are positive qualities to all three of the openings to the Higher responses. Example 1 spends some time contextualising the extract (explaining how it fits into the novel as a whole), and, while this is useful, the student does not really address the main focus of the question – the mood and atmosphere created – but instead discusses the behaviour of the characters in an engaged way. The points made are supported by selected detail, but the response could be much more focused on the question.

Example 2, on the other hand, establishes a clear overview from the very start, and maintains this focus on the creation of mood and atmosphere throughout the rest of the response, selecting and highlighting detail, and discussing words and phrases in order to support the points made about the mood and atmosphere. This response has made the most promising start.

Example 3 starts with a rather general observation, never actually pinning down what the mood and atmosphere are, and discusses what is happening in a similarly general way, without developing points, or making much of the selected detail.

Both of the Foundation responses show an awareness of what is going on in the extract, and both show empathy for Francis and refer to the situation he is in. Example 4 uses selected detail from the extract more effectively than Example 5, which means that it is the more effective of the two.

Putting it into practice

Read the responses to the extract from *Heroes* again, together with the comments on them. Now look at the opening sentences you wrote for the mood and atmosphere/ thoughts and feelings question you chose for one of your prose texts, in Activity 3.

How would you rate what you wrote, comparing it with the levels of response in the examples?

- to develop confidence in responding to prose extract questions by selecting details from the extract

Selecting details from the extract

GradeStudio

Examiner tips

- On your first readings, when you are selecting detail, it's a good idea to find something from the beginning, something from the middle, and something from the end of the text, then fill in between. That way you're more likely to cover the whole of the extract.
- Never neglect the beginning or end of an extract – there's a good reason why it starts and ends as it does!
- Make sure each piece of selected detail is linked to your overview (your main point, or 'take' on the question).

Activity 1

Selecting and highlighting detail is one of the key factors in achieving grade C or above. It's important to be as thorough as possible.

The following activity will help you in selecting and highlighting detail.

1 Go back to the extract you chose for either character or mood and atmosphere in the previous activities. Underline, or jot down, words and phrases that would support your overview (your 'take' on the question).

2 Make a grid similar to the one below, and complete it with words and phrases from the extract you chose, and an explanation of how they are effective.

This grid is for the extract from *Heroes*.

Word/phrase	Effect
'A heat wave gripped… the air.'	Heavy, oppressive slow-motion movie imagery; sense of time having slowed down
'For three days…'	Highlights Francis' determination, yet helplessness
'haunted'	Suggests Francis' constant, unnerving presence
'standing across… looking up'	Suggestive of stalker
'venturing… might catch a glimpse'	Tentative, cautious
'no one came or went'	Sounds final, particularly positioned at end of paragraph – yet he persists
'Nicole's father… during those times.'	Again highlights Francis' sense of isolation and caution
'A small boy… rode his bicycle endlessly'	Seems like almost the only movement – effective contrast with Francis' stillness
'bogey man'	Link with 'haunted'?
'Yes, I wanted to say… avoiding even in my mind'	Again suggests sense of isolation and helplessness
Final few lines describing small boy	Sense of finality – Francis left alone again. Even the child has found him unnerving.

Heroes

A heat wave gripped Frenchtown, the heat almost visible in the air. People moved as if in a slow-motion movie, gathering on front lawns and piazzas in the evening after the shops closed, hoping for a breeze to cool them off. Men walked slowly as they went off to work in the shops as weary-looking in the morning as they were late in the day, after their shifts were over.

For three days, I haunted Sixth Street at all hours, standing across the street and looking up at the second floor of Nicole's house, venturing sometimes into the yard, hoping that I might catch a glimpse of her coming or going or at a window. Despite the heat, the piazza on Nicole's second floor tenement remained vacant. The windows were open to allow cooler air to enter the tenement but no one came or went.

Nicole's father left the tenement to go to the shop just before seven o'clock in the morning and returned shortly after five in the afternoon and I avoided him, kept away from the street during those times.

A small boy in the house across the street from Nicole's rode his bicycle endlessly on the sidewalk and gazed at me occasionally as I waited. Finally, squinting against the sun, he asked: 'Why are you here all the time?'

I shrugged. 'Waiting.'

'Are you the bogey man?' he asked, scratching his chin.

Yes, I wanted to say. A kind of bogey man who does terrible things like letting his girl get hurt and attacked, purposely avoiding even in my mind that terrible word: what had actually happened to her.

The boy waited a moment for my reply then pedalled back into his yard, silent as he gazed at me over his shoulder. He went into the house and did not come out again.

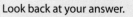

Activity 2

The following activity will help you develop your ideas into a full response on an extract.

1 Choose another extract from one of your prose texts (about a page in length).

2 Decide which type of extract question you would like to practise (either character, or mood and atmosphere/thoughts and feelings) and write your own question.

3 Before you start writing your answer, jot down notes on the following points:
   - What is your response to the question?
   - Which words and phrases from throughout the extract could you use to support the points you are making? It may help to underline these words and phrases, to make sure you are covering the whole extract.
   - How do your selected words and phrases work to help you understand the character or mood and atmosphere?

4 Now put it all into practice, and write your answer to the question you have devised.

GradeStudio

Check your answers

Look back at your answer.
- Have you started with a clear focus on the question?
- Have you kept your focus on the question throughout your answer?
- Have you selected and highlighted detail from throughout the extract?
- Have you linked your selected details to the points you want to make?

My learning objectives ▼

● to develop confidence in responding to prose extract questions by understanding how to answer the question effectively

Answering the question effectively

Below is an extract from *Paddy Clarke Ha Ha Ha*. The novel is about a ten-year-old boy (the Paddy Clarke of the title) growing up in Ireland in the 1960s. In this extract, he is playing outside with his friends when an accident happens.

Paddy Clarke Ha Ha Ha

Our territory was getting smaller. The fields were patches among the different houses and bits left over where the road didn't meet properly. They'd become dumps for all the waste stuff, bits of wood and brick and solidified bags of cement and milk bottles. They were good for exploring but bad for running in.

I heard the crack, felt it through my foot and I knew there was going to be pain before it came. I had time and control to decide where to fall. I fell onto a clean piece of grass and rolled. My cry of pain was good. The pain was real though, and rising. I'd hit a scaffolding joint hidden in the grass. The pain grew quickly. The whimper surprised me. My foot was wet. My shoe was full of blood. It was like water, creamier. It was warm and cold. My sock was wringing.

They were all standing around me. Liam had found the scaffolding joint. He held it in front of my face. I could tell it was heavy, the way he was holding it. It was big and impressive. There'd be loads of blood.

– What is it? said Sinbad.

– A scaffold thing.

– Thick eejit.

I wanted to take my shoe off. I held the heel and groaned. They watched. I pulled slowly, slowly. I thought about getting Kevin to pull it off, like in a film. But it would have hurt. It didn't feel as wet in there now, just warm. And sore. Still sore. Enough for a limp. I lifted my foot out. No blood. The sock was down at the back, under the heel. I took it off, hoping. They watched. I groaned again and took the sock away. They gasped and yeuched.

It was brilliant. The toenail had come off my big toe. It looked cruel. It was real. It was painful. I lifted the nail a little bit. They all looked. I sucked in breath.

– Aaah – !

I tried to put the nail into its proper position but it really hurt. The sock wasn't going to go back on.

They'd all seen it. I wanted to go home now.

Read the extract then look at the two examples of student responses.

Example 1 is a Foundation response to the question:

What do you think of the way Paddy speaks and behaves here? Give reasons for what you say, and remember to support your answer with words and phrases from the text.

Example 2 is a Higher response to the question:

With close reference to the extract, show how Roddy Doyle creates mood and atmosphere here.

Read the two student responses, keeping in mind this checklist of points:

- [ ] Clear focus on the question
- [ ] Thorough discussion of the extract
- [ ] Reference to the novel, to put the extract in context
- [ ] Selection and highlighting of detail to support the points made

Example 1

When reading this extract, my first thought was that Paddy is a young and naive boy who just wants to impress his friends. This is shown at the end of the extract when Paddy says, 'They'd all seen it. I wanted to go home now.' This suggests that even though it was 'Still sore' he was going to stay in the fields to show his mates that 'The toenail had come off' his big toe. Paddy is then trying to impress his friends again when he is just groaning and not crying with agony. This is shown when Paddy says, 'My cry of pain was good. The pain was real though.' When reading this extract I also feel sorry for Paddy, because nobody should have to endure an accident like that and then feel like they have to show their mates. I think this is very sad.

Example 2

Roddy Doyle creates a very anxious mood in the extract. When it starts off saying that their 'territory was getting smaller', it gives you a sense of foreboding and draws the reader in to discover what is going on. Paddy describes the scene as though he is on some sort of brilliant adventure, although he reminds us that he is just a child full of curiosity when he mentions 'exploring'.

Doyle increases the tension and eagerness to read on when Paddy 'heard the crack'. Doyle then makes Paddy show a great deal of understanding for a ten-year-old boy when he predicts that there 'was going to be pain'. Paddy also shows his need for control when he claims that he 'had time and control to decide where' he fell. When Paddy exclaims that his 'cry of pain was good' after he fell, the reader then understands that Paddy is just playing around.

Doyle describes Paddy as knowing that the 'pain was real' but Paddy is not really all that bothered. He is more interested in how 'impressive' he has been to his friends and how cool and brave he will look if there is 'loads of blood'. Doyle then adds to the eerie sense of foreboding when Paddy starts to 'slowly, slowly' take off his shoe. Paddy does this for added effect and makes the scene try to be 'like in a film'.

Although Paddy is upset when there is at first 'no blood', the reader feels a sense of relief that Paddy hasn't injured himself too much. However, when Paddy 'took the sock away' the reader is as shocked as Paddy's friends are when Doyle describes how 'The toenail had come off' and 'It was painful'. This helps the reader create sympathy for Paddy, even if he does think that 'It was brilliant'.

However, when Doyle describes how Paddy starts to realise how serious the injury is by claiming that it 'really hurt', Paddy forgets that he looks brave and 'impressive' and he simply claims that he 'wanted to go home'.

Example 3

In this extract Paddy is playing with his friends and "hit[s] a scaffolding joint hidden in the grass" and suffers "real pain" as a result. Paddy describes vividly his pain and his feelings and emotions, through the stream of consciousness style, feeling somewhat privileged to have "the toenail come off [his] big toe."

At the start of the extract Paddy is referring to the fields he and his friends play in as "our territory" and how it is "getting smaller." As the Corporation houses are being built, Paddy and his friends will have fewer places to play. This brings about quite a sad mood to Paddy's thoughts, as his familiar surroundings start to disappear from his life. He describes the fields as "dumps for all the waste stuff." He says "they [are] good for exploring but bad for running in." Later in the extract he certainly proves that.

Paddy hears "the crack." He feels "it through [his] foot and knew there was going to be pain before it came." The aural and pain related description makes the atmosphere more intense, as we can now easily empathise with Paddy and his feelings of pain. The atmosphere sustains its theme of pain and suffering. Paddy's "cry of pain" is described by Paddy as "good" and "real". Paddy is experiencing pain and discomfort but to an extent, he enjoys the pain and seems to find it thrilling and exciting, unaware as to what will happen through the course of his injury. This strange outlook on pain and discomfort can somewhat confuse the reader, and makes the mood more exciting, as Paddy doesn't spare us any details on his experience. Paddy tells us that all his friends were "standing around [him]" Liam "[finds] the scaffolding joint" and "held it in front of [Paddy's] face. Paddy "could tell, it was heavy, the way [Liam] was holding it." Paddy is impress[ed] by the "big" scaffolding joints and assumes there will be "loads of blood." The mood of the extract changes as Paddy no longer seems to be in pain in a negative way, but in a positive way, like he is impressed by his injury and is experiencing a rush.

This mood soon changes as Paddy cannot "take his shoe off" as he "want[s] to." He [holds] his heel and groans." Again, we empathise with Paddy as he "slowly" pulls off his shoe as his friends are watching and he can't show too much pain, wanting to appear tough. The atmosphere is very intense as Paddy describes his "sore" foot. Paddy reveals disappointedly that there is "no blood" present. But, Paddy reveals a "cruel" vision of his toenail which had "come off." Paddy seems very proud as his friends "gasp", "yeuch" and "suck in breath."

Paddy's mood of excitement then instantly changes. His foot "really hurt[s]" and his "sock wasn't going to go back on." After all his friends had seen it, he now "wanted to go home." The abrupt closure of the extract leaves a curious atmosphere. Will Paddy be OK? What will happen to him? The questions mount up and we wish to read on.

MOVING UP THE GRADES

GradeStudio

How to go up the grades

Example 1 has a clear focus right from the start, and the student selects relevant details to support the valid points made. However, there is no real system to the approach: for example, the first reference to the text is to the ending of the extract. As a result, this response is underdeveloped, and would get a mark representing a high D. To get a better mark, thorough tracking through the extract, selecting words and phrases throughout, would have been advisable.

Example 2 has a clear focus from the start and works through the extract sensibly, selecting and highlighting relevant details to support the points made. The use of short quotations, integrated within the student's own words, is good practice, as it's a waste of time to copy out big chunks of text. Another strong point is the way that the student has tracked through the text from beginning to end. This thoughtful and thorough discussion would get a mark representing B. To get to A or A* it would have been useful for this student to have focused more on the *effects* of specific words and stylistic features.

Example 3 is well focused, analytical and evaluative throughout. The contextualisation of the extract in the

Putting it into practice

Now look at the practice response to your own prose text. How would you rate what you wrote, comparing it with the levels of response for the answers above?

opening of the response is a sensible way to start, as is the reference to 'how' in the first paragraph. This makes for a well-focused beginning to the response. As well as being sensitive to Paddy's experience and his reactions, the student shows real appreciation of how Doyle has created specific effects, such as in, 'Paddy hears "the crack."' He feels 'it through [his] foot and knew there was going to be pain before it came.' The aural and pain related description makes the atmosphere more intense, as we can now easily empathise with Paddy and his feelings of pain. The changing mood and atmosphere is carefully tracked through the extract (look at the references to 'mood' and 'atmosphere' throughout the response) with well-selected supporting evidence – quotations are again brief and integrated within the student's own words. These qualities would get this response a mark representing A*.

Anita and Me, by Meera Syal, is about a young Asian girl growing up in a mainly white village in the Midlands in the late 1960s. In the extract below the central character, Meena, has become separated from her friend, Anita, in a place the local children fear.

Activity 2

Read the extract, then make notes in answer to the following exam-style question:

With close reference to the extract, show how Meera Syal creates mood and atmosphere here.

Anita and Me

At first I could see nothing; the darkness had a texture so dense I fancied my outstretched hands were pushing against giant elastic cobwebs. The ground under me conspired to disorientate me. It was spongy and silent under my uncertain feet, no crackling branches or noisy heather to reassure me that I walked on the earth and owned it; I felt this forest now owned me. After slapping head-first into a few low branches I became accustomed to the gloom and began to pick my way more confidently through the trees, fixing my gaze on the back of Anita's shoes which seemed to glow like low, uneven landing lights.

Then I suddenly realised that I could not hear the fairground any more. It had been replaced by a much louder noise, a low breathing made up of night breeze, whispering leaves, insects humming in morse code and the sporadic mournful hoots of a lone high owl.

'Hee-yaar!' whispered Anita, who came from nowhere to appear next to me and yanked my hand, pulling me after her up a pebbly rise until we were looking down at an immense black hole, which I only realised was water when I saw the moon suspended in its centre, a perfect silver disc in what looked like another upside-down sky.

'Hollow Pond!' I breathed reverently.

I had been here once before, I have a vague memory of sitting at the water's edge with someone, papa maybe, listening to him explain how this old mine shaft had filled with water and formed a natural pool. But I was not to ever swim there because it led into a huge labyrinth of other shafts and was therefore bottomless, unforgiving. There must have been a time when Hollow Pond was open to the village as I could not imagine papa sneaking around and snagging his trousers on some barbed wire to get in. But of course, since Jodie Bagshot's drowning, no one ventured here anymore.

GradeStudio

Getting the grade!

Here are two students' responses to the exam-style question on page 53. Read the answers together with the examiner's comments.

C grade answer

Student 1

The opening of this extract begins with 'At first'. This instantly gives the reader a clue that something more is to come. This could perhaps create a mood of tension and apprehensiveness, as the reader will be intrigued and will want to read on to find out what comes next. •————

> General awareness

The third sentence, beginning 'It was spongy and silent', is a very long sentence with three different punctuation marks, a comma, a semi-colon and a full stop. The use of long sentences and punctuation creates a mood, as the reader will read on faster and because of this, tension is built. •————

> Only a glimmer of awareness – simple spotting of features

Meera Syal's choice of vocabulary is very descriptive. She uses lots of adjectives to describe the scene that Meena and Anita are in. Because of the intense adjectives and very descriptive language, the reader can and will believe the situation. The perhaps eerie but exciting mood created will perhaps put an exact picture in the reader's mind, which is perhaps Syal's intention, to directly involve the reader. The main sentences portray this mood of mystery but yet wanting to pursue the questions of the mind. In this part Meena is delving deeper into the surroundings of the hollow pond, and likewise the reader is intrigued and will delve deeper into the novel to find out more:
'Then I suddenly realised that I could not hear the fairground any more. It had been replaced by a much louder noise, a low breathing made up of night breeze, whispering leaves, insects humming in morse code and the sporadic mournful hoots of a lone high owl.'

> General

> Vague and general

> Unnecessarily long quotation

The words 'suddenly realised' create atmosphere, and tension is built, because of the word 'suddenly'. This word is sharp and there is a change in mood; up until this point Meena can hear the fairground. Now 'suddenly' she cannot. The use of this could perhaps make the reader want to read on. •————

> Selects and comments

> Aware of change in mood and atmosphere, though awkwardly dealt with

In conclusion, Meera Syal creates mood and atmosphere by the mysterious tone of the extract. The long sentences and lots of punctuation also create a tense mood, the language and word choice that Syal uses is very descriptive and engages the reader, and therefore this will also create a mood and atmosphere. •————

> Mainly general conclusion

Examiner comment

Although Student 1 shows some awareness of mood and atmosphere, recognising its tension and mystery, the context is not made very clear, and too much time has been spent with simple spotting of features, such as sentence lengths and punctuation marks. This has consequently got in the way of the student showing an understanding of how the words and images actually work. As it stands, this response would get a mark representing a low C, at best.

A* grade answer

Student 2

Meera Syal creates mood and atmosphere by describing the area around the Big House as almost magical and enchanting. •————— **Overview/insight**

The extract begins with 'At first I could see nothing'.

This creates the feeling of Meena feeling completely lost and ready for anything unexpected. •

'The darkness had a texture so dense.' This makes the wood seem like it is able to swallow her up into its darkness. •————— **Selecting and highlighting detail**

'Giant elastic cobwebs' makes the woods seem untouched, forbidden, that is why no one has been here, the cobwebs are still there. •————— **Closely read**

Meena is not sure where she is going – 'my uncertain feet' – she is simply following Anita, and is not sure about anything tonight. She is not allowed to be here, and her feeling of foreboding increases her curiosity. •————— **Clear about context**

'I felt this forest now owned me' – she feels she has been swallowed up into the darkness, as if she is a prisoner there. •————— **Inference**

She knows she has stepped too far into the heart of the forest to turn back: 'I could not hear the fairground any more.' Instead she begins to hear 'a low breathing', which shows how scared she is. This form of personification shows how Meena has turned the sound of the night breeze into the sound of, maybe, an animal, waiting for her in the dark. •————— **Style and effect**

'Insects humming in morse code and the sporadic mournful hoots.' She has created the imagery of this forest being alive, her brain is playing mind tricks. •————— **Astute**

'…whispered Anita.' Meera Syal makes the characters whisper, even though there is no one else there who would be listening to them.

'Immense black hole…' makes the scene feel mysterious. The way Meena describes the hole shows her fear, of maybe falling into it. •————— **Valid inference**

'… bottomless, unforgiving.' Once you fell into 'Hollow Pond' you were trapped forever.

Meena has taken a huge risk to be here: 'I could not imagine papa sneaking around and snagging his trousers on some barbed wire to get in.' This shows Meena's forced entry, and how eager she is to get there. •————— **Understanding**

She knows that a girl died here, drowning, but still had to explore: 'Since Jodie Bagshot's drowning, no one ventured here any more.'

She wants to have experienced being in the forest at night, it is a huge adventure for her. •————— **Sensitive**

The characters are ready, and daring. They are confident at first, but when they are in the forest they feel panicky. The setting is mysterious and magical. The experience feels unreal, like a dream. •————— **Secure overview for conclusion**

Examiner comment

This response starts with a clear and confident overview, and then proceeds to analyse the extract in detail, really probing the effects of the words and phrases used and always relating this back to the overview of the extract. There is also a much clearer sense of the context of the extract here. It would get a mark representing A*.

MOVING UP THE GRADES

How to go up the grades

Student 1 could have achieved a better grade with less empty spotting of features and more focus on how words and phrases contribute to the overall mood and atmosphere of the extract. Student 2's response is sensitive and appreciative and reveals plenty of evidence of analysis and evaluation.

Putting it into practice

Look at the two examples and write down a list of the features that earned Student 2 the better mark. From this list, make a list of targets for yourself, to improve your performance in responses to extracts from your prose texts.

Improving your responses

The extract below is from *A Christmas Carol* by Charles Dickens. The novel is set in Victorian London and tells the story of Ebenezer Scrooge. He is initially a hard-hearted man but, through a series of supernatural experiences, he changes his attitude and puts an end to his money-hoarding ways. The extract is from near the beginning of the novel, and describes the atmosphere in London one December night. The extract has been annotated (as you may annotate the extracts from your set texts in the exams).

Sense of being lost – so dark and foggy, torches are needed to show the way

A Christmas Carol

Personification of church tower and bell – highlights extreme darkness and cold

Human figures suggest poverty

Personification of water and ice: 'sullenly' and 'misanthropic' sound as if everything is working against humans

More contrast – sense of excitement and activity

Meanwhile the fog and darkness thickened so, that people ran about with flaring links, proffering their services to go before horses in carriages, and conduct them on their way. The ancient tower of a church, whose gruff old bell was always peeping slyly down at Scrooge out of a gothic window in the wall, became invisible, and struck the hours and quarters in the clouds, with tremulous vibrations afterwards as if its teeth were chattering in its frozen head up there. The cold became intense. In the main street, at the corner of the court, some labourers were repairing the gas-pipes, and had lighted a great fire in a brazier, round which a party of ragged men and boys were gathered: warming their hands and winking their eyes before the blaze in rapture. The water-plug being left in solitude, its overflowing sullenly congealed, and turned to misanthropic ice. The brightness of the shops where holly sprigs and berries crackled in the lamp heat of the windows, made pale faces ruddy as they passed. Poulterers' and grocers' trades became a splendid joke: a glorious pageant, with which it was next to impossible to believe that such dull principles as bargain and sale had anything to do. The Lord Mayor, in the strong-hold of the mighty Mansion House, gave orders to his fifty cooks and butlers to keep Christmas as a Lord Mayor's household should; and even the little tailor, whom he had fined five shillings on the previous Monday for being drunk and blood-thirsty in the streets, stirred up to-morrow's pudding in his garret, while his lean wife and the baby sallied out to buy the beef.

Foggier yet, and colder. Piercing, searching, biting cold.

Abrupt sentence to emphasise the point

Sense of light within the darkness – hope? cheer?

Contrast in colours and shop windows

Minor sentences in a short paragraph on their own – emphasise return to darkness and cold

Overview – overwhelming sense of darkness, coldness, and perhaps mystery, only briefly relieved by flashes of colour/human activity

The following activity will help you to see how careful selecting and highlighting of detail can lead to developing a clear overview of the extract, and show how a specific mood and atmosphere is created.

Activity 1

Read the extract and the comments around it, then jot down your ideas in response to these questions:

- What is the main mood and atmosphere in this extract? Sum it up in a few words.
- If this extract were to be illustrated, what colours would be most effective? What may this suggest about the mood and atmosphere?
- What is the effect of the personification of the church bell and the water/ice? How may this add to the overall mood and atmosphere?
- What about the people in the scene – how do they add to the mood and atmosphere?

GradeStudio

Examiner tips

In writing responses to questions about the mood and atmosphere/thoughts and feelings of an extract, you will improve your answer if you:

- start strongly
- make sure you are selective in highlighting short phrases (or just words) from the extract that support your point of view
- aim to look at the extract as a whole, and don't get bogged down in looking at it sentence by sentence in isolation.

Read the following responses written by two students to the extract from *A Christmas Carol*, printed on page 56. They wrote in answer to the question:

With close reference to the extract, show how Charles Dickens creates mood and atmosphere here.

When you have read both responses, think about the following points:

- Which student has established a clear overview, by focusing on the mood and atmosphere created in the extract?
- Which student has highlighted specific words and phrases, and fitted them into his or her overview?
- Which student do you think would get the better mark here?

Example 1

Charles Dickens begins by describing the fog and the darkness. He describes the 'gruff old bell' in the church tower as 'always peeping slyly' at Scrooge but in the fog it 'became invisible, and struck the hours and quarters in the clouds'. He almost gives the bell a life of its own, and personifies it as an old man, watching people carefully in the 'ancient tower'. Charles Dickens continues this when describing the cold. He writes that the bell rang with 'tremulous vibrations' and gives it life again by saying 'as if its teeth were chattering in its frozen head'. It makes you think of an old man, hidden by the clouds, with his shivering in the cold being the bell ringing. It is a very good way to show both the age of the church and its bell, as well as the fog and the cold. He then describes the cold becoming intense, more powerful, making people grateful for any source of warmth. He says that 'a party of ragged men and boys were gathered: warming their hands and winking their eyes before the blaze in rapture'. The phrase 'in rapture' is used to show that the cold has made the discovery of fire truly blissful for the group of men and boys.

The water-plug is 'left in solitude' and the overflow is 'sullenly congealed'. These phrases are also making inanimate objects into people with emotions; 'sullenly' is a word that makes you think of a child sulking, and 'left in solitude' describes the child's friends leaving. In this case the 'friends' are the labourers, who have gone to warm themselves by the fire. The overflow turns to 'misanthropic ice'.

The mood changes quite a lot after that, as it switches from describing the rather spooky darkness and fog to a busy street, full of light and heat: 'The brightness of the shops where holly sprigs and berries crackled in the lamp heat of the windows, made pale faces ruddy as they passed.' The light is glowing red and orange and reflects off people's faces, making 'pale faces ruddy'.

Charles Dickens creates mood and atmosphere very effectively by personifying objects and using metaphors to describe the fog and cold.

Example 2

The author begins by creating the image of a wild, rough, unforgiving night. Dickens uses phrases such as 'the fog and darkness thickened' to show that the night was such that you couldn't see, and anything could be waiting for you. He extends this mood by describing the 'gruff' bell of the 'ancient' tower 'peeping slyly' down on Scrooge, so he couldn't see it. Dickens uses vocabulary such as 'gothic' to further the mood of tension. The author describes people huddling around a fire to escape the bitter cold. They are said to be 'ragged' and 'in rapture' at the 'blaze'. The author begins to create a sharp contrast between the warmth and security of the fire, and the cold, hostile night. This is continued throughout the passage – a sentence about the waterpipe 'sullenly' freezing is followed by a description of the 'brightness' of the shops. This sentence contains lots of Christmas connotations (such as 'holly', 'berries crackled') to show that it is the season that has this effect on the world, and the effect is huge. Words such as 'splendid' and 'glorious' are used to build up the atmosphere of holiday cheer being an oasis in the harshness of London.

Dickens describes two Christmases – one of the wealthy Lord Mayor and his fifty butlers and cooks, and one of a poor tailor, who is normally 'drunk and blood-thirsty' but is also caught up in the spirit of Christmas. This shows that the mood affects anyone.

To finish, the author reverts to describing the cold and fog to remind the reader that the Christmas cheer is only temporary.

GradeStudio

Check your answers

If you chose Example 2 as the better response, that's the right answer. Although both these answers have responded in detail to the extract, and have selected and highlighted details to support their ideas, Example 2 gets off to a better start, by establishing an overview ('a wild, rough, unforgiving night'). This enables the student to place subsequent observations within the overview. In Example 1 the student picks out appropriate parts of the text, but tends to deal with them in isolation, and sometimes just spots features, as in the final sentence of the response.

Example 1 is thorough and quite thoughtful, so it would earn a mark representing a low **B**, whereas Example 2 is representative of **A*** work, because of the close focus on *how* the highlighted details create the mood and atmosphere specified in the first sentence.

If you were to give advice to Student 1 on how to improve his or her answer, what three things would you suggest?

The following extract is from *Ash On A Young Man's Sleeve* by Dannie Abse. This semi-autobiographical novel is based on the author's experiences growing up in Cardiff in the 1930s. The extract is from the start of the novel.

Ash On A Young Man's Sleeve

June the first was our agreement, our day of peace. It came in that year with all sunshine and the windows open and the neighbours' radio. It was tennis-players and the yellow seasick trams grinding down Cathedral Road. It was the end of a school day where we left our carved initials, hurt and momentous, in the wooden desk, and school teacher (old Knobble-knees) rubbing off chalk from the blackboard like a nasty day from the calendar. 'Mind how you cross the road,' she said. 'Please, Miss Morgan,' asked Philip, 'can I have my yo-yo back? I won't talk again during lessons.'

Keith had asked me to his house for tea, for it was our day of peace, an interlude in our constant campaign of being mean to each other, of masterful vilification. We walked hardly together for we were enemies. Suddenly Keith said, 'There'll be bananas and cream, so you can leave as soon as you've eaten 'em.' 'I like bananas and cream,' I said. Other people's houses have a strange smell. Keith Thomas's home was no exception and I was sniffing. 'What's the matter?' Keith's mother asked. 'Is there something burning?' I went very red when the others sniffed. They just stood there, Keith and his mother, heads cocked, drawing air through their nostrils. 'I can't smell anything,' she said. I could.

Perhaps it was the odour of sin or the past remains of previous tenants. I ate bread and butter and jam and Welsh cakes, and Keith sniffed and sniffed louder and louder, quite ostentatiously I can tell you.

'Blow your nose, Keith,' said his mother. I tipped the tea over the tablecloth and grew redder…

This was all a long time ago: I was ten years high and I lived in South Wales. There everything was different, more alive somehow.

The following activity will give you further practice in selecting apt details in order to form an overview of mood and atmosphere.

Activity 3

The question on this extract is:

With close reference to the extract, show how Dannie Abse creates mood and atmosphere here.

1   As you read the extract, make a note of words and phrases that help create mood and atmosphere.

2   Look back at the words and phrases you have chosen, and see whether you can generalise about the mood and atmosphere.

3   Choose from the following list the three words that you think best match the mood and atmosphere of the extract:

tense, exciting, nostalgic, childlike, happy, mysterious, embarrassed

4   For each of the words you have chosen from the list, gather together words and phrases from the extract that support your choice.

5   Finally, explain to a partner why you think the words and phrases you have chosen fit the adjectives you have selected from the list.

The following activity will help you improve your techniques for answering character-based extract questions.

The extract below is from *Resistance* by Owen Sheers. This is a novel set in Wales during the Second World War, which imagines that Britain has been invaded by the Germans. The extract features Sarah, one of the central characters, whose husband, together with the rest of the men from their isolated valley, has left to take part in a resistance movement.

Activity 4

Read the extract, then make notes in answer to the following exam-style question:

With close reference to the extract, show how Owen Sheers suggests Sarah's feelings here.

Resistance

It was her birthday, however much she'd tried to forget it. She hadn't mentioned it to any of the other women and she'd tried not to even mention it to herself. There was, she felt, nothing to celebrate. Twenty-seven years old. Childless. Abandoned in a world gone sour. Just the afternoon before she'd ridden Bess up on the hill and watched a pair of crows circle and dance about each other in the air. When they'd landed they'd rubbed shoulders and Sarah had felt again, as if for the first time, the pain of her solitude. Even the carrion crows who ate the eyes of her dead ewes had companionship while she, as ever, had just the blood-pulse of the wind in her ears and the heat of Bess's neck to keep her company. Not for the first time, she'd wanted Tom dead. Not because of what he'd done, but instead of what he'd done. In death he would have given her an answer. She would have known where he was. As it was, she just had nothing. Even the women whose husbands had gone to war, they'd always had something: letters, days of leave.

She'd once seen a crowd of these women down at the station in Pandy. They were wearing their best dresses, their cheeks rouged and their lips bright red, waiting for a train to take them into Newport. There, they would wait on the platform for the fast train carrying troops from the training fields of west Wales up to London and the ports of the south coast. The train didn't stop at Newport, just gave a couple of blasts on its whistle and steamed on through. But these women always went to watch it pass, dressed as if for a dance. Just for the chance of seeing the faces of their husbands, their lovers, as the long line of carriages clattered and rushed past them trailing its heavy plume of steam. It was often a hopeless journey but the women still went, just for the chance, that glimpse. But Sarah didn't even have that. There was nowhere she could go in the hope of seeing Tom. No reports she could read with her heart in her mouth. And no letters she could wait for. Just an empty vigilance for some sign, some hidden message and her long rides up on the hills, forever facing up to their blank answer.

GradeStudio

Getting the grade!

Here are two students' responses to the exam-style question on page 61. As you read the responses, together with the examiner's comments, think about to what extent the students have used the detail of the extract to focus on the question.

C grade answer

Student 1

In this extract Sarah is feeling sorry for herself, because it is her birthday and she feels there is 'nothing to celebrate'. The way it says 'Twenty-seven years old. Childless.' suggests some of the reasons she feels sad. It is as if she is listing the things she is unhappy about. It also describes how when she rode up into the hills even the crows seemed to have a better life than her, because they were 'a pair'. This suggests how much she is missing her husband when even a pair of crows remind her of how alone she is.

She goes on to think about how she resents Tom being away, because she has no idea of where he is and what he is doing, and remembers seeing groups of women going to Newport station in the hope of catching a glimpse of their husbands and lovers on their way to war. She can't even do this, because Tom is in the resistance and she doesn't know whether she'll ever see him again and can't even say goodbye. It's as if she is jealous of these other women at the station, 'But Sarah didn't even have that.'

At the end of the extract there are a lot of negative words: 'Nowhere she could go', 'No reports she could read', 'No letters she could wait for', 'empty vigilance', 'blank answer'. These words and phrases suggest how negative and depressed Sarah is feeling, although a birthday should be a happy time.

- Focus on the question
- Awareness of thoughts and feelings – comment on style
- Sensitive awareness and empathy
- Apt reference
- Valid inference
- Some discussion of language and effect

Examiner comment

Student 1 focuses on the question, and selects and highlights some apt details to support the points made. There are some flashes of real insight, such as the reference to the significance of the crows, the women at the station, and the use of negatives, but these are not developed sufficiently to take this response out of grade C.

Student 2

The writer suggests Sarah's feelings through her birthday. This is a time when she should be happy, but he tells us that she feels there is 'nothing to celebrate' and that she 'hadn't mentioned it' to any other women, as if she felt happiness was not to be allowed or shared. He uses short, bleak sentences such as 'Childless' and 'Abandoned in a world gone sour' to show us her thoughts. He also shows us the 'pain of her solitude' by telling us of a 'pair of crows' that 'circle and dance' and make her feel alone without a partner. He uses these birds to show us just how alone she really is as these crows she envies for their companionship are carrion crows, which 'ate the eyes of her dead ewes'. Again, Sheers returns to the short staccato sentences that follow her train of thought, her longing to know what has happened to her husband, because at least if she knew that he was dead, she would have 'known where he was'. This seems to show Sarah's religious feelings also, as it seems to say that if he was dead, she would know he was in heaven.

Sarah also seems to envy the women whose husbands are away at war. The writer shows this by telling how Sarah has seen a 'crowd of these women' at the train station, waiting to catch a glimpse of husbands or lovers on the train steaming past. The writer gives the reader a glimpse of this hope, but shows the reader that Sarah has no hope by telling us that she does not even have hopelessness, she has nothing.

At the end of the extract, the writer again uses abrupt sentences to show the reader Sarah's thoughts and, in turn, feelings. He repeats the word 'no' to show that Sarah's life has become a nothingness void of any meaning, love or happiness. 'No reports she could read', 'no letters she could wait for'. Again the writer shows her feelings of emptiness, writing that even the last thing she has, her 'vigilance' for a 'sign', or 'some hidden message', even her 'long rides up on the hills' are 'empty' for her, and that her feelings, and her search for an answer are 'blank'.

Annotations (right margin):

- Focused discussion
- OK, but could develop
- Focus on detail – but missed opportunity to probe further
- Getting onto style and effect
- Perhaps
- Sensitive response
- Language and effect
- Sensitive – getting towards an overview

Examiner comment

Student 2 looks closely at words and phrases and their effects. This is a sensitive response that carefully selects and discusses the details of the extract. As a result, it would get a mark representing a low grade A.

GradeStudio

Student 3

The author effectively suggests Sarah is feeling alone, slightly bitter and almost lifeless. — *Confident overview and focus*
He suggests she is lifeless by writing how she wants to forget her birthday, which should be a joyous occasion. 'It was her birthday, however much she'd tried to forget it.' This indicates that Sarah is so depressed or feeling unloved that she wants to forget the day she was brought into the world and given life. This is also backed up when the author says there is nothing to celebrate. 'There was, she felt, nothing to celebrate.' This effectively shows Sarah wants to forget or live someone else's life. — *Point well made*

It is suggested Sarah feels bitter because the writer notes down a few facts of Sarah's life that show she has achieved nothing and possibly has no one. 'Twenty-seven years old. Childless. Abandoned in a world gone sour.' It is suggested that Sarah feels lonely because of the one-word sentence, 'Childless.' This one sentence strongly indicates how Sarah feels alone as she wants a child, someone of flesh and blood, but does not have one at her increasing age. — *Style and effect*

When Sarah watches the crows, the author describes her loneliness in a different way. He suggests that Sarah longs for her husband as she watches the two crows, feeling, 'as if for the first time, the pain of her solitude'. Watching the crows brings back Sarah's pain at Tom abandoning her but it also stirs up anger within her. 'Not for the first time, she'd wanted Tom dead.' This shows her anger at the man she loves for abandoning her without so much as a goodbye. Feelings of uncertainty are also brought up with this anger at Tom as she does not know whether he is dead or living or what he may be doing. 'Even the women whose husbands had gone to war, they'd always had something: letters, days of leave.' — *Sensitive evaluation of characters and relationships*

The passage describes Sarah's fading hope and her helplessness. It talks about the women with husbands at war and how they go to the station to try to see them but the passage also talks about Sarah's lack of hope of ever seeing Tom again. 'There was nowhere she could go in the hope of seeing Tom.' In this one sentence it suggests Sarah can believe Tom is dead or never coming back to her. While there is a lot that suggests Sarah has lost all hope, the — *Well-developed evaluation*
last sentence of the passage shows Sarah still has waning hope. 'Just an empty vigilance for some sign, some hidden message and her long rides up on the hills, forever facing up to their blank answer.' While this does suggest hope, it could also be interpreted as Sarah riding up with no hope but to simply deny the feelings of helplessness and aloneness she has. — *Perhaps*
The writer suggests Sarah's feelings of helplessness and aloneness. The writer suggests Sarah's feelings of hope go up and down, but the author effectively communicates the fact — *Personal interpretation*
Sarah knows Tom isn't coming back without saying it as a simple fact.

Examiner comment

Student 3 has a particularly clear overview and focus in the first sentence, and this prepares the ground well for the remainder of the response. Again, this is an effective response to the extract, and details are carefully selected and thoughtfully discussed. This answer would get a mark representing a clear A*.

How to go up the grades

There are high quality skills in the responses of Student 2 and Student 3. Both of these are sensitive and personal responses to the extract, and use well-chosen details from the text to support their ideas, although neither student picks up on the possible symbolism of the carrion crows being associated with death, which would have further extended their understanding. Students 2 and 3 both display qualities associated with the highest grades (sensitivity, overview, evaluation, close focus on how the extract is written) but the opening of Student 3's response just gives it the edge. Student 1 shows clear awareness of Sarah's thoughts and feelings, and has selected some apt details to support the points made, but would need to develop the ideas in more detail, and focus more on the effect of specific words and phrases (for example, the use of minor sentences for 'Twenty-seven years old. Childless' and the way the effects of the way the women at the station are described), in order to move out of grade C to grade B or higher.

Putting it into practice

Look at the examples of student writing above, and write down five reasons why Students 2 and 3 achieved higher marks than Student 1.

Peer/Self-assessment

Now look at your written response to an extract question focusing on character. How does it compare with the work of Students 1, 2 and 3 on pages 62-64?

You could carry out the steps below on your own work, or swap with a partner, looking at each other's written responses.

- Annotate the response in the same way as the examiner annotated the student's responses.
- Now try to grade the answer, using the mark scheme in 'Moving up the grades' on page 137.
- Write down three things that would improve the quality of the response.
- Looking at your own work, decide which skills you have developed and used successfully in this response.
- Which skills do you need to develop further?
- Plan how you will achieve the improvements that have been identified as appropriate to your own work.

GradeStudio

Examiner tips

Remember, in the exam you will have 20 minutes to answer the extract question.

2.2 Prose essay questions

In Unit 1 you will answer one out of a choice of two questions on the 'different cultures' prose text you have studied, and in Unit 2 you will answer one out of a choice of two questions on the other prose text you have studied (either contemporary prose or literary heritage prose).

The pattern of questions will be similar for all prose texts in both units. The following questions are typical of the questions you are likely to see in your exams.

Higher tier questions

On the Higher tier you will find questions on **character** (there is always at least one character-based question on each text), such as:

▶ Write about the relationship between ... and ... and how it is presented.

▶ What do you think of ... and the way he/she is presented to the reader?

▶ Imagine you are .... At the end of the novel, you think back over its events. Write down your thoughts and feelings. Remember how ... would speak when you write your answer.

▶ In your opinion, who or what had the greatest influence on ...? Support your answer with detailed reference to the text.

▶ Show how ... is affected by ....

▶ To what extent is it possible to feel sympathy for ...? Remember to support your answer with detailed reference to the text.

▶ How is the character of ... important to the novel as a whole?

▶ Show how and why the character of ... changes throughout the novel.

▶ To what extent ... (is someone responsible, etc.)?

You will also often find questions on **theme**, such as:

▶ How does ... present the theme of ... in ...?

and questions focusing on the **title**, such as:

▶ Why do you think ... called the novel ...?
▶ To what extent do you find ... an effective title for the novel?

and questions focusing on **specific incidents or places** and their importance, such as:

▶ How is ... important to the novel as a whole?

These are the assessment criteria that you will be assessed against.

Assessment Objectives:

AO1 Respond to texts critically and imaginatively; select and evaluate relevant textual detail to illustrate and support interpretations.

AO2 Explain how language, structure and form contribute to writers' presentation of ideas, themes and settings.

AO4 Relate texts to their social, cultural and historical contexts; explain how texts have been influential and significant to self and other readers in different contexts and at different times.

Foundation tier questions

Typical question patterns on the Foundation tier include ones on **character** (as on the Higher tier, there is always at least one question for each set text about a character or characters), such as:

▷ What do you think of …? Think about …

▷ Write about the character of … Think about …

▷ Imagine you are … At the end of the novel you think back over its events. Write down your thoughts and feelings. You may wish to think about …

▷ What do you think about …? Give reasons for what you say.

▷ For whom do you have the most sympathy? Give reasons for your choice.

You will also find questions about **theme**, such as:

▷ Write about … in the novel. You may, if you wish, focus on two or three specific incidents where … is important.

and questions focusing on the **title**, such as:

▷ Why do you think … chose the title … for the novel? Think about …

and questions that focus on specific parts of the novel (e.g. funny/sad/moving/most interesting parts), as well as questions about **places**, such as:

▷ What impressions do you get of … Think about …

character

theme

title

place

GradeStudio

Examiner tips

- Questions on the Foundation tier tend to be similar in focus to those on the Higher tier, but will be more simply expressed, and are more likely to have bullet points to guide you.

- **If an essay question has bullet points, it's important to use them to provide a framework for your answer – and to write as much as you can on each bullet point.**

- In the exam you will improve your answer if you focus closely on the question. Students often find it helpful to underline the key points of the question, to make sure that their focus is clear. Demonstrate this focus in your answer by repeating vocabulary used in the question.

Finding your way around your prose texts

GradeStudio

Examiner tips

- In the exam you need to be able to quickly bring to mind key details from your set texts.
- You need to select and highlight key details to support the points you want to make.
- Examiners are always impressed by someone providing a clear overview of the text!

In all types of essays, it's important to provide an overview of the whole text. This means being able to sum up its essence, or key points, as briefly as possible.

The following activity will help you develop an overview of your prose texts.

Activity 1

Working on your own or with a partner, try to summarise the key points of one of your set prose texts in as close to 50 words as possible.

Read this example of a 50-word summary of *Of Mice and Men* to give you an idea of how this may be achieved:

> Friends Lennie Small, who's strong, and George Milton, who's smart, arrive at a ranch in Soledad, a place of dreams and loneliness. When Lennie kills first a mouse, then a puppy, then a woman, George has to shoot him, in a final act of friendship. Their dreams die with Lennie.

Now write your own 50-word summary. Try to include an overview of the key events, mention of the most important characters, and reference to the important themes.

However well you know the 'story' of your prose text, you also need to know your way round it, so that you can select and highlight what is most important for you to respond to in the question you are answering.

The following activity will help you organise your thoughts about the most important parts of your prose texts.

Activity 2

1. Working individually or in a small group, divide the story of your chosen prose text into five episodes. It may help you to imagine your chosen text is to be serialised in five instalments, and to think about what the key event would be in each one.

2. Choose one of the five key episodes, and make a list of the most important characters involved in it, and how they are behaving.

3. Make a note of which themes or messages from the text are represented in your chosen episode, and how they are treated in it.

4. Choose a key quotation to represent your chosen episode.

5. Share your results with the rest of the class. You may choose to present your ideas in the form of a poster, and explain them. Keep your poster and refer back to it to remind yourself of the sequence of events in your prose text.

Writing in the voice of a character

In the exam you may be asked to imagine you are a character from the prose text. You may be asked to tell the story of the novel, or prose text, from the character's point of view at some point after the end of the story, or you may be given a specific focus, such as giving your feelings about particular events or characters. To make a successful answer, you need to think about the characters in detail – how and why they behave as they do at different points in the novel or prose text, how they feel about other characters, and how they may reflect important themes.

Remember, in the exam you could be asked about **any** character, so don't just focus on the same character all the time in your practice answers.

The following activity will help you think about characters and the ways in which they may be interpreted in depth.

GradeStudio

Examiner tips

If there is a question asking you to imagine you are a character from your prose text, you will improve your answer if you:

- use specific details to show you know the text well
- discuss the behaviour of other characters thoughtfully and sensitively
- 'sound' like the character – use the type of language he or she would use
- include reference to key themes.

Activity 3

1 Working either on your own or in a small group, choose a main character from the prose text you are studying.

2 Write down the following points about your chosen character, and note key quotations that support them:
- the first time the reader meets the character (or hears about him/her), and the impressions you get from this
- five key points in the story for your character
- how your chosen character may highlight the important themes of the novel
- things others (including, if relevant, the writer) say about the character, and what these show
- things the character says about himself/herself, and what these show
- the last time you see the character – and the significance of this.

3 Choose one quotation that you feel sums up your character, and explain why.

4 Present and explain your ideas to the rest of the class.

The following activity will show you how the same events may be interpreted in different ways by different people. It will also give you practice in selecting and highlighting relevant details.

Activity 4

1 Choose an important part of your prose text, where something significant is taking place that involves several of the most important characters. It may be a whole chapter, or part of a chapter.

2 Decide on the characters you think are important in the part of the novel or prose text you have chosen.

3 Taking one character at a time, make a note of what their thoughts and feelings are likely to be about what is happening. Think about what has happened before (and keep in mind what you, as the reader of the whole text, know will happen afterwards).

4 Select the main points of the episode you have chosen from each character's point of view. Think about how other characters are speaking and behaving, and what this character would think of them. You may also be able to identify themes or messages from your prose text that are evident in your chosen part.

5 Write a few paragraphs from the point of view of each of the characters.

Getting the grade!

Read the following two responses from Foundation tier candidates to a question on *Pride and Prejudice* by Jane Austen. This novel tells the story of the Bennet family, and the efforts of the mother, Mrs Bennet, to find suitable husbands for her daughters, despite Mr Bennet's apparent lack of enthusiasm.

The students are writing in response to this exam-style question:

Imagine you are Mr Bennet.

At the end of the novel you think back over its events. Write down your thoughts and feelings.

You may wish to think about:

- **your relationships with your daughters**
- **your opinions of your daughters' marriages**
- **your relationship with your wife**
- **anything else you think important.**

E grade answer

Student 1

Ah what a lovely time that was. This past year has been unforgettable – we had our ups and downs but it all turned out well in the end. But alas my wife is still with us. That stupid woman would do well to read a few books, but never mind, my daughters are all faring well, especially Elizabeth and Jane for they are both married to such wealthy and respectable men, unlike Lydia who ran off with Mr Wickham – such a terrible business that was but thanks to Mr Darcy we sorted it out properly without having to resort to fisticuffs. The only daughters still with us are Kitty and Mary but I feel that Kitty will soon be wed to a wealthy friend of Darcy's. I feel we may never lose Mary and her dreaded piano playing.

- Very general – some voice
- Simple sense of characters and relationships
- Reference to events
- Detail
- Nice touch of humour – reference

Examiner comment

Although there is a simple sense of the main characters and their relationships in this response, it is underdeveloped, and as no detailed knowledge of the text is evident, it could not reach a grade C. Although the topics in the bullet points have been referred to, they have not been used as a framework on which to build the response. As the answer is so brief, and the awareness of characters and relationships is only just touched on, the mark here would be representative of a high grade E.

Student 2

Well, these past few months have been rather eventful, have they not? I do miss Lizzy most terribly now she is wed. And what a surprise, finding out her affections for Mr Darcy! Him, of all people. My, I remember that first ball, they came back ever so spirited but so distressed over Mr Darcy. In her usual way, of course, Elizabeth appeared not to care at all and made merry with her sisters.

> Nice sense of Mr B

> Aware of characters and relationships

> Apt reference – could develop

> Sense of character

Mrs Bennet certainly hasn't lost <u>her</u> spirit, she still flaps away over guests and her dear Lydia. Lydia... Well, what can I say? She has got her own way through and through and I must be happy for her. But still I have a constant feeling of regret and bitterness over what came to pass in that respect. If only I'd listened to my dear Lizzy; I still clearly remember her warning to me, cautioning against Lydia's reckless behaviour. We have been thoroughly deceived on more than one account.

> Aware of Mrs B

> Aware – but could have been developed

However, thanks to Elizabeth's recent acquirance of an admirer, the problem was resolved. And now we have just two girls unmarried and one still at home. I feel indefinitely that although they have gained, Mrs Bennet and I have lost out. We have lost two of our most deserving daughters to marriage and another of her own will. But, indeed, I have gained three excellent sons-in-law, each equally as promising in money as in love; although Wickham is less so.

> General

> Detail?

> A bit general – some awareness

We have to thank our relatives, the Gardiners, for a great deal. They have been extremely useful in our affairs and faithful friends. Perhaps I shall write again to them. We have had so many letters of congratulations these past weeks! We are bombarded. Of course it is an excitement for Mrs Bennet each day. But we hear such pleasant things.

> Picking up again

> Aware – but lacks detail

> Good sense of Mr B again

I have advised my cousin Mr Collins to think about revising his loyalty regarding Lady Catherine de Burgh and her nephew. I know not yet what action, if any, he has taken. Lizzy was rather shaken after her somewhat unwelcome visit from the lady herself. All in all, however shocking and tense the events have been, I am satisfied with the way things have turned out, and although my favourite daughter is gone away and Mrs Bennet continues to complain loudly about her nerves, I am pleased for them all and very proud.

> Reference

> Rather general, but apt conclusion

Examiner comment

This response has a clear awareness of characters and relationships, which is evident not only through the references made but also through the convincing 'voice' – it sounds like Mr Bennet. Although there are references to key events in the novel, these tend to be rather underdeveloped. On balance, therefore, this response would receive a mark representing C+. Had there been more specific detailed reference to the text, this could have earned a higher mark.

GradeStudio

Getting the grade!

Read the following response to a question on the novel *Silas Marner* by George Eliot. This tells the story of a weaver, the Silas Marner of the title, who is betrayed and misunderstood and, as a consequence, becomes an isolated miser. After all his savings are stolen, he adopts an abandoned child, Eppie, who restores his faith in humankind and reconnects him to the people around him. Read the student's answer together with the examiner's comments.

The student is writing in response to this exam-style question

Imagine you are Silas Marner. At the end of the novel you think back over its events. Write down your thoughts and feelings. Remember how Silas Marner would speak when you write your answer.

A* grade answer

Student 3

I'm but a simple man living and breathing, yet I had to learn something and there be no one to disbelieve that.

> Clear sense of Silas and his character

I remember her golden curls on the hearth, how beautiful they were to me, but sadly all for a different reason. I should've had nothing to do with them ol' coins, they're enough to destroy a man. I knew from then she were mine. 'I'll keep her 'till anyone can prove they've a right to her.' She came to my door wanting warmth and comfort and yet I found that in her.

> Detail

> Key point

> Direct reference

> Sensitive – a lovely point

She'd be mine forever, we'd need only a simple home and simple things though I wish I could've given her more. Our Eppie deserved the world; I couldn't give her it. I thought that Master Cass was being a grand neighbour until that day. The day I got me gold back, odd really but it seemed I could never have both my money and Eppie, 'That's God's work.' Now Master Cass said that he was Eppie's father even though it were me she'd been calling that name ever since she could talk. He were going to take her away from me but she wouldn't go. I told her 'you must go'. He could give her plenty more than I, yet she wanted me.

> Sensitive to characters and relationships

> Interesting

> Echo

> Characters and relationships

I'd have nothing though without Dolly, she were the only one to speak a word with me in 16 years of living in Raveloe. She were so nice, said all the stories of me were nonsense, stories I hadn't heard but it seemed no one but Dolly thought any more of me than them in Lantern Yard. She's quite a mother, and so proud of young Aaron (as am I!). Dolly used to tell him the stories of me, but she must've been the only one to end them with 'such nonsense as I'm ashamed to speak of'.

> Good interpretation of detail

> Detail/overview

> Lovely use of detail – really getting into character

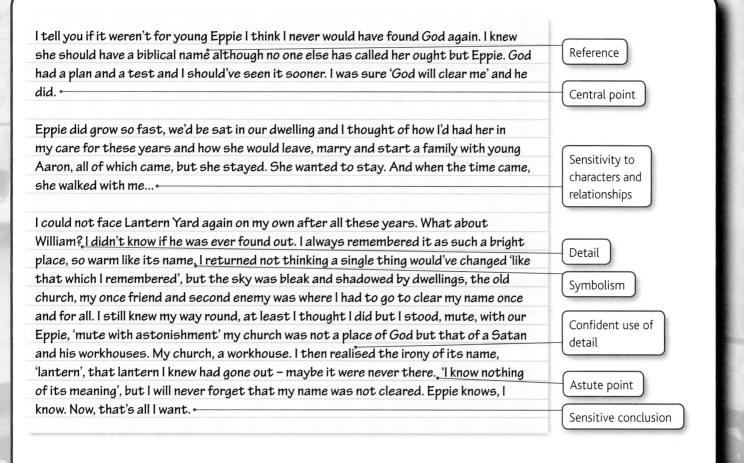

I tell you if it weren't for young Eppie I think I never would have found *God* again. I knew she should have a biblical name although no one else has called her ought but Eppie. God had a plan and a test and I should've seen it sooner. I was sure 'God will clear me' and he did. — Reference / Central point

Eppie did grow so fast, we'd be sat in our dwelling and I thought of how I'd had her in my care for these years and how she would leave, marry and start a family with young Aaron, all of which came, but she stayed. She wanted to stay. And when the time came, she walked with me... — Sensitivity to characters and relationships

I could not face Lantern Yard again on my own after all these years. What about William? I didn't know if he was ever found out. I always remembered it as such a bright place, so warm like its name. I returned not thinking a single thing would've changed 'like that which I remembered', but the sky was bleak and shadowed by dwellings, the old church, my once friend and second enemy was where I had to go to clear my name once and for all. I still knew my way round, at least I thought I did but I stood, mute, with our Eppie, 'mute with astonishment' my church was not a place of God but that of a Satan and his workhouses. My church, a workhouse. I then realised the irony of its name, 'lantern', that lantern I knew had gone out – maybe it were never there. 'I know nothing of its meaning', but I will never forget that my name was not cleared. Eppie knows, I know. Now, that's all I want. —

Detail / Symbolism / Confident use of detail / Astute point / Sensitive conclusion

Examiner comment

This is a sensitive and convincing interpretation of Silas' character. It contains key points from throughout the novel, including its conclusion. The student has succeeded in showing a detailed knowledge of the text by including references to other characters and some important events. There is also a clear understanding of the messages and themes of the novel, and reference to some of its symbolism. Because of these qualities, this response would receive an A* mark.

How to go up the grades

MOVING UP THE GRADES

Although all three of the responses to questions involving writing as a character show awareness of characters and relationships, and knowledge of the text, only the student writing on *Silas Marner* has really taken the opportunity to show a good knowledge and understanding of the novel, and has managed to refer to more subtle points, such as themes and symbolism.

Putting it into practice

You have now read three responses to questions involving writing as a character. Working with a partner, or in a small group, compare the approaches of these three students in their responses.

Consider the following qualities:

- detail
- voice (does it sound convincing, from what you know of the novel?)
- discussion of characters and relationships
- references to themes/imagery.

Writing about your opinions of characters

In the exam you may be asked to give your opinions on one or more characters. To help you answer successfully, you need to know which parts of the novel or prose text are significant to the character or characters you are writing about. You need to show your understanding of the ways in which each character is important to the story as a whole. It is also important to discuss his or her relationships with other characters. If you can show an understanding of how characters highlight the story's themes, this will improve your answer even more.

The following activity will help you organise your thoughts about a character from one of your prose texts.

GradeStudio

Examiner tips

- In the exam it makes a real difference if you make an impact with a strong opening to your response.
- Aim to refer to the question in the first few sentences of your response.
- If you can sum up your chosen character's role in the novel, and link that to the question, you are giving an overview of the text, which is a **high-level skill**.

GradeStudio

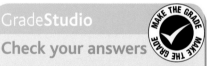

Check your answers

- Does the paragraph make a strong, clear point in the first sentence?
- Does it show an overview of the character's role in the story?
- Have points been linked back to the question?
- Does the paragraph give a good idea of the direction the rest of the response is going to take?

Activity 1

1 Working on your own, or with a partner, choose three or four of the main characters in one of your prose set texts.

2 Then, quickly write down a list of points about each character – there's no need to think too much at this stage, just make sure you make as many points as possible.

3 Next, choose one of the characters, and organise your list of points into sections. For example, there could be a section on first impressions, one on important events, one on relationships with others, and one on final impressions.

4 The next stage is to make sure you have short but key examples of direct reference to support your points. This could be in the form of short quotations, maybe just a word or two, or in the form of very specific reference – with exact names of places or people, for example.

5 You now have the basic foundation for a response, so try writing an introductory paragraph to the question:

What do you think of … and the way she or he is presented in the novel?

The following activity will help you write an answer giving your opinions on the importance of a specific character.

Activity 2

1 Working on your own or with others, choose a key character from one of your prose set texts.

2 Make notes on the following points:
- key events that your chosen character is involved in
- how your chosen character affects the events of the story
- how your chosen character relates to other characters – affecting the way they behave, for example
- how your chosen character highlights, or makes the reader aware of, the themes of the text.

3 Share your findings with the rest of the class.

4 Write a plan for a response to the following question (fill in the name of your chosen character):

How is … important to the novel as a whole? Use the notes you made earlier to help you organise your answer.

5 Develop your plan into a full response – probably about 3–4 sides long.

To Kill a Mockingbird, by Harper Lee, is set in the deep south of the US in the early 20th century. It tells the story of events in the small town of Maycomb, from the point of view of a young girl, Scout Finch, whose widowed father, Atticus, is taking a courageous stand by defending a black man accused of the rape of a white woman. The cook in the Finch household, Calpurnia, has an important role in the family, and in the community.

On the next page are three extracts from student responses to the exam-style question:

How is the character of Calpurnia important to the novel as a whole?

First, look at the openings of the students' responses.

Example 1

Calpurnia is very important in the novel because not only is she a mother figure for Jem and Scout, but she gives the reader and the Finch family a link to the 'negro' race.

Calpurnia is very much a part of the Finch family. She is described at the beginning of the novel as 'the cook', but as the novel progresses, we discover that she is much more than that. Since Atticus' wife died some years before, Cal has looked after Jem and Scout while Atticus is at work and clearly cares for them. For example, she makes Scout her favourite crackling bread on her first day of school. Although at the beginning of the novel, Scout says, 'I had felt her tyrannical presence my whole life', by the end, Scout has come to realise that Calpurnia is a very good person and is only firm with her because she cares about her.

Example 2

'To Kill a Mockingbird' is a novel set in the 1930s in Alabama by Harper Lee, which focuses upon the trial of a black man for rape and the lives of Scout and Jem. Calpurnia is the cook to the Finch family, and well educated (although her grammar can be 'erratic') but is often perceived as being closer to the family than most black servants at the time. Indeed, Atticus says she is a 'valuable member of the family' when criticised by Aunt Alexandra for how he treats Cal. She is a valuable part of Jem and Scout's lives, and although Scout describes her presence as 'tyrannical', she learns many important lessons from Cal.

Example 3

In 'To Kill a Mockingbird' Calpurnia is seen as the mother of the children. Even though Calpurnia is black this makes no difference to how Atticus and the children treat her. I think that Calpurnia is the symbol of racism and segregation in 'To Kill A Mockingbird' because she lives freely without ridicule in both worlds. I think the main reason why Calpurnia is no different, to the children, from any white person is because of Atticus. Atticus believes that you cannot judge someone until 'you put on their skin and walk around in it', and he teaches this moral to Jem and Scout. I think this is why they accept people so readily into their lives no matter who they are.

GradeStudio

How to go up the grades

All three examples have their strengths, as they all show knowledge and understanding of the novel. However, the one with the best focus on the question of 'importance to the novel as a whole' is Example 1, as the student gives a clear opinion from the first sentence, provides a clear overview, and supports points with detailed reference to the text. Example 3 also makes interesting points, but does not have quite the same tight focus on the issue of Calpurnia's importance as Example 1. Example 2 is a focused discussion of Calpurnia and the world of the novel, but would benefit from more reference to the question.

Putting it into practice

Now look again at your introduction – the opening sentences on the character you chose to write about in Activity 1 page 74. How does it compare to these three examples? If necessary, try re-drafting or rewriting it, to ensure that it refers clearly to the question, shows detailed knowledge of the text, and is clear and coherent.

Now we will look at the key points each student makes in answer to the question:

How is the character of Calpurnia important to the novel as a whole?

Example 1

I think Calpurnia is important to the novel because she breaks down the line of segregation running through Maycomb. The first time we see her cross this line is when she takes Jem and Scout to her church.

Example 2

With regard to the black community, Calpurnia could be said to represent a 'bridge' with two different lives – her life with the Finches and her life with the black community. This is shown when the children visit the black church. Cal's speech patterns are different, as noticed by Scout (it is here that she learns not to flaunt an education) and she is protective of the children with Lula (emphasising her motherly qualities). Cal is a respectable cook in white society, but the Negroes hold mixed views, Lula mocking her by calling her 'Miss Cal'. Calpurnia's son, Zeebo, also holds different positions in the black and white communities, a 'garbage collector' to the whites and a 'choir leader' to the blacks. Indeed, Cal is so much of a bridge that Atticus takes her with him to tell Helen about Tom's death, emphasising the level of respect he has for her.

Example 3

Calpurnia helps Jem and Scout understand about racism and the injustice black people face as well as showing the reader. When she takes the children to church, we realise how poor the black community is, and how little respect the white people have for the black church. White people gamble in it on weekdays, only leaving it on the weekends for the blacks to worship in it. We also learn about how uneducated the black population is. Calpurnia is one of only four of the congregation who can read and write, one of the others being Zeebo, Calpurnia's son, whom she taught to read herself. However, no matter how inconvenienced they are, the black community makes the best of what they have, for example, singing hymns by 'lining' and decorating their simple church with coloured broken glass.

GradeStudio

How to go up the grades

All these examples are paragraphs making reference to a key point in the novel in which Calpurnia is involved: she takes the children to her own black church, where white people rarely, if ever, go. Example 1 starts off with an excellent overview about Calpurnia breaking down segregation, and provides apt support (the example of their visit to the church), but unfortunately the student does not develop the paragraph by explaining what happens and how it is significant in showing Calpurnia's importance to the novel as a whole. Example 2 contains much more detailed reference to the text, although there is a tendency for the student to say everything he or she can recall about the church visit without necessarily making it relevant to the question. There are some very useful points here, but they could have been expressed in a more focused way. Example 3 shows a real awareness of the impact on the reader, which is a high-grade skill, and includes succinct references to relevant details. There are strong qualities to all three; a blend of the best qualities from each would make an outstanding paragraph.

Now we will look at the conclusions the students wrote at the end of their responses to the question:

How is the character of Calpurnia important to the novel as a whole?

Example 1

For these reasons, I think that Calpurnia is greatly important to the novel as a whole, the most important one being that she introduces the Finch children to the black community. I think this is one of the main reasons why Jem and Scout are not racist, despite being surrounded by racist views in Maycomb.

Example 2

I think that Calpurnia is also very important to the children. When Scout gets into a fight with Walter Cunningham, Jem invites him back for dinner. Scout is rude about the way he eats and that's when Calpurnia steps in. This shows that Calpurnia not only loves them but also helps Atticus discipline them and teach them morals, a job I'm sure no 'normal' black servant would ever be allowed to do. I think this shows that Calpurnia is one of the most important characters as she shows that segregation laws are absurd.

Example 3

Overall, Cal's purpose is to provide moral and social teachings, to represent a bridge between black and white society, and to act as a mother figure to Jem and Scout.

GradeStudio

Check your answers

Look back at your answer.
- Have you focused on the question and given an overview of your chosen character's importance?
- Have you made specific references to the text?
- Have you made reference to the question in each paragraph?
- Have you summed up your main points in a clear conclusion?

GradeStudio

How to go up the grades

Again, there are positive qualities to all three of these conclusions. Example 1 has a confident tone, although perhaps its focus is rather narrow. The final sentence is also rather over-assertive, as it ignores the influence of the children's father, Atticus. However, this is a valid point of view. Example 2 is a strong personal response, but introduces new ideas/incidents that really should have been dealt with earlier in the response. Example 3, although very brief, does the job of a conclusion well – it summarises the key points made in the rest of the response, and reminds the reader of the overview that has been formed.

Getting the grade!

Look at the following responses to a question on Jack, a character from *Lord of the Flies*. The novel is about a group of boys who land on an uninhabited island after a plane crash, and tells how their attempts to create a society on the island are fraught with conflict and arguments, which eventually lead to violence and chaos. Read the responses, together with the examiner's comments.

The students are writing in response to this question:
What do you think of Jack and the way he is presented in the novel?

D grade answer

Student 1

The character of Jack is presented in several different ways throughout the novel. He starts out as the innocent lost schoolboy that you would expect, though the situation they are put into has a strong effect on him and his actions reflect this.

> General

> Why?

> All a bit vague, but some focus

Jack is firstly introduced into the novel as a harmless yet somewhat feisty and strong-willed young boy. When the boys are faced with the situation of choosing a leader for their group, Jack instantly puts himself forward, his bribe being that he was head of choir at home and would therefore be the perfect leader. The rest of the boys fail to be convinced by Jack and instead they believe the only reason Jack wants to be leader is so that he can get his own way. This causes tension in the group and results in the two strongest characters, Ralph and Jack, falling out.

> Much more assured – supported judgements

The groups of boys split into two smaller groups. Jack is the leader of one group and Ralph is the leader of the other. Ralph wants to move the fire to the top of the mountain in the hope of being rescued. On the other hand, all Jack wants to do is hunt beasts to survive – it does not appear that his focus is on being rescued. It comes across as though Jack doesn't care about being rescued. The arguments between the groups become worse and worse so the groups decide to separate completely and to work alone.

> Valid references, but lacking development and detail

Jack's attitude seems to have influenced the boys in his group and their group seems to evolve around hunting for survival. Ralph's group focuses on the more important things like being rescued. Jack's group therefore threatens to kill Ralph's group on Jack's commands, showing once again how Jack has influenced some of the boys.

> Ends very suddenly, without any specific reference to events

Examiner comment

There are positive points to Student 1's response – a focus on the question, an emerging overview in the comment on the overall view of Jack, and a sensible starting point for the discussion on the readers' first impressions, although this could have been a lot more specific. There are few references to specific events, however, particularly from the later stages of the novel, and an examiner would be left wondering exactly how well the student knew the novel. Because of these qualities, this response would get a mark representing grade D+.

GradeStudio

During the novel we hear a lot about Jack and the way he is presented as an anarchist who stands for the right to do what he wants and for a society without rules.

Focus and overview

We first meet Jack Merridew when he arrives marching with the rest of the choir. The fact that he is leading them in the march suggests that he is used to being obeyed as the leader and enjoys the feeling. The marching also implies that he likes to impose military type ideas into situations where it wouldn't be expected. This idea is also shown when he agrees with Ralph about making rules for the sole reason of punishing those who break them. Overall, as head of the choir, he is presented as arrogant especially when he says 'I ought to be chief!' which implies he expects everyone to agree with him immediately and can't imagine the boys not doing what he says.

Good focus – evaluating behaviour

Well supported judgements

The next important point we learn about Jack's character is that he is sadistic and cruel because he argues with Ralph over keeping the fire going because he is obsessed with hunting the pigs. This is shown when the first thing he says after they conclude the island is uninhabited is, 'You need an army for hunting.' This shows it is the first thing he thinks about, implying he is violent and is pent up with anger which shows why he wants to hurt and kill. Even when some others agree with Ralph that starting a fire in an attempt to get rescued seems like a better idea he doesn't agree. This shows he is irrational and authoritarian because he would rather govern himself, even though he is only a child.

Developing evaluation, with plenty of evidence

I think that Golding also tries to present Jack as quite charismatic. Although it may not seem that way at first, he manages to persuade many of the boys to join his tribe of hunters despite the fact that many of them agreed to begin with that the fire was more important. This shows that he managed to change their minds, possibly by manipulating the truth, to gain control. This is shown when he asks rhetorically whether anyone really cares about rules, showing again how he would rather allow the group to fall into anarchy than let someone else say what to do. I think that Golding may have wanted to represent Jack as the original beast that tempted Eve in the Garden of Eden. There are many religious symbols in the novel, most predominantly the character of Simon, who is the spiritual heart of the book, shown almost as Jesus the martyr when he is killed. I think that the way Jack tempts the boys into hunting and tyranny represents the devil that destroyed the paradise in the Bible. This is a very powerful symbol, showing Jack as a very evil character.

Focus on author's presentation

Good point to support speculation

Apt reference

Speculating about symbolism

The major event that presents Jack as a cruel and evil character is the death of Simon. The part he plays in his death is large and he seems to show no remorse afterwards. This can be shown by the fact that after he has murdered Simon he decides that they should 'Steal the fire' from Piggy. This shows that he feels what he did was acceptable but I think that it also implies that he has begun to see sense in the fact that they can't survive on the island for ever and eventually they will need to be rescued. I think that this presents Jack as slightly more rational after the death of Simon but in no way sorry for what his tribe has done.

Key reference

Thoughtful and evaluative

The final part of the novel that presents Jack's character is the scene when Piggy is killed after attempting to appeal to Jack's 'appeal for justice'. In this scene Piggy is knocked over a cliff and killed when he hits the beach. Jack's reaction to this is delight that the conch,

Key reference

the symbol of order, is broken, and he can declare himself leader. This shows that Jack is sadistic and cruel because he shows pleasure in a child's death and also because he is so overcome with power that he feels he can appoint himself leader. This is despite the fact he originally felt the need to vote and for everything to have rules, (even if only to punish those who break them). This shows that the anarchy that he instigated has finally taken him over and his innocence has been completely destroyed by the events that have taken place on the island. •————————————————— Overview

Overall, I think that Jack is presented as a leader in the novel; however, his kind of leadership is dictatorship or anarchy rather than diplomacy. The events such as the murder of Simon show him to be cruel and sadistic and he eventually becomes completely overrun with power after the death of Piggy. I think that he represents temptation in the book and he is ultimately the reason that the boys lose their innocence. Just as 'The Beast' is the reason the Garden of Eden was destroyed, showing that the island and its inhabitants could be interpreted as representing the story of Genesis in the Bible's Old Testament. •————— Confident conclusion

Examiner comment

Student 2 maintains the confident overview and focus established from the very start of the response. This is an evaluative and well supported discussion of the character, and would get a mark representing A*.

How to go up the grades

There are positive points to both the responses to the *Lord of the Flies* question, but, despite quite a good introductory paragraph, Student 1's answer is not nearly as developed as that of Student 2. It is important to show detailed knowledge and understanding of the whole text, and this is what Student 2 has done.

Putting it into practice

Look again at the notes you made in preparation for a question of this sort (*What do you think of …?*), and the introductory paragraph you wrote. How well prepared were you to write the sort of response that would get the best possible mark? You may want to go back and develop your notes further, before extending them into a full practice essay.

GradeStudio

Examiner tips

Remember, in the exam you will have 40 minutes to answer the essay question.

Writing about your judgements of characters

Another type of character question may give you a choice of characters to write about through, for example, asking which character you have the most or least sympathy for. You should give some thought to this before the exam.

The following activity will help you write an answer to a character question in which you are asked to give your opinion on a character and how they are presented.

GradeStudio

Examiner tips

● Foundation tier candidates are more likely to be asked: **What do you think of … and the way s/he speaks and behaves at different points in the novel?**

● For questions on the presentation of a character or characters, all you need to think about is what the writer's ideas about the character may have been, so look at the way the character speaks and behaves, relates to others, the language used to describe him or her, and the effect of this, and the way the character may highlight the themes of the text.

● A handy tip is to think about whether the character is contrasted with another character or characters, and the effect of this.

Activity 1

1 Decide on the character in your text for whom you feel the most sympathy. For example, you may decide to choose someone who has little control in his or her life, or someone who experiences a lot of problems, or someone who is misunderstood. It helps if you can give a strong reason, so consider your choice carefully.

2 Jot down some ideas on your chosen character:

   • why you've chosen him or her
   • the first time your chosen character appears or is mentioned in the text, and how that affects your feelings towards him or her
   • important moments in the story for your chosen character
   • the relationships your chosen character has with other characters
   • the last time your chosen character is seen (or referred to) and how this affects your feelings towards him or her

   Finally, sum up your main points about the character.

3 Now, write the first paragraph of your response to the question:

   For which character do you have the most sympathy? Give reasons for your choice, and support your answer with detailed reference to the text.

4 Swap your opening paragraph with that of a partner.

5 Discuss the strengths of your response with your partner and then talk about areas that need improvement.

The following activity will help you clarify your thoughts about characters in your set novels.

Activity 2

1 Working on your own or with a partner, choose two characters from one of your set prose texts: the one you have the most sympathy for, and the one you have the least sympathy for.

2 Taking these characters one at a time, decide why you have the most or least sympathy for him or her. This information will form your overview.

3 Choose parts of the text that support your judgements, making sure that you have examples from throughout the text.

4 Share your ideas with someone else who has chosen the same character(s), if appropriate.

5 Write the first couple of paragraphs of your response to one of the following questions (fill in the name of your set text):

Which character in ... do you have the most sympathy with?

Which character in ... do you have the least sympathy with?

You may later decide to complete this task by writing a full essay.

GradeStudio

Examiner tips

● With this sort of question, Higher candidates will probably be asked to show how the writer's presentation of the chosen character creates sympathy (or lack of it) for him or her.

● Both Foundation and Higher tier candidates need to remember to support answers with detailed references to the text.

● Remember, so long as you give clear and valid reasons for what you say, you can't be wrong – your choice of character may well be different from other people's choices, so be confident in your own judgements.

● Throughout your answer, make sure that you keep making reference to the question (the word 'sympathy' or 'sympathise', should occur regularly, probably in every paragraph).

On pages 84–85 are two student responses to this type of question, where they have been asked to choose which character they want to write about.

As you read these responses, look out for the following points:

☐ Clear focus on the question

☐ Thoughtful discussion of the chosen character

☐ Discussion of the chosen character's relationships with other characters

☐ Evidence of detailed knowledge of the text

In Example 1 the student is writing in response to a question on *About a Boy*. This novel, by Nick Hornby, tells the story of how the narrator, Will, befriends a boy called Marcus, and how each of them helps the other to come to terms with their life. The task here is:

About a Boy tells the story of Marcus and the story of Will. Which of these stories interests you the more, and why?

Example 1

Of the two main characters, personally I feel that Will's story is of more interest to me. Perhaps most importantly, he is a character that I can identify the most with, but also he develops more profoundly throughout the book and almost becomes the unknowing, yet reluctant 'hero'.

The first impression of Will is that he is a 'cool' character. He has plenty of money, knows how to dress, doesn't care about anything and does exactly what he wants, when he wants. Most people would be envious of this carefree lifestyle, and the way in which Will does not have to comply with any rules, or go to a day to-day job. It is of particular note, also, that he does not seem to realise how much of a 'big deal' to other people his lifestyle would be – having had such an easy time all through his life he is particularly complacent about this, so doesn't really care about anything, or realise what the real world is like. However, he pays a great deal of attention to keeping in the know, and being up-to-date with what he perceives to be 'cool' and modern, as well as making sure that his music taste (notably Nirvana) is up-to-date, and just what all the magazines say you should be listening to. However, it is quite interesting to me how fake his life seems to be – he has absolutely no perception of reality, takes no responsibility for anything and lives his life out of magazines. From this, you can see how, despite the fact that he is a fully grown man with all this money and luxury, his life is certainly still lacking perhaps the most important part of life – other people.

However, despite first impressions of a selfish, arrogant man, later on Will demonstrates that he does actually have more depth and compassion than is first seen. We see, as the book develops, that Will develops a sense of meaning and purpose as well as emotions towards Marcus. This complete shock to the system causes him to be dragged back to reality – finally he develops his personality to that of a fully grown adult, however slowly it does ultimately happen. This extrovert child completely changes the way Will views the world, and however much he begrudges that fact, his buried affection for him gradually surfaces: even Rachel thinks that Marcus really was Will's son, so much has Will's personality changed.

You also see how he manages to interact with other human beings much more effectively as time passes on. He stops lying to people, realising the incredibly damaging effect it has, and even when it comes to Marcus's mother Fiona (who he'd contemptuously written off as a crazy, hippie-like woman who isn't worth knowing) Will does begin to realise that she is doing the best she can for her son, and while she isn't getting it right every step of the way, she is not actually such a bad person. Essentially, he learns to empathise with those who are not as fortunate as him, and this is instrumental in turning his life around – his womanising stops, he is able to settle down with a woman he has genuine feelings for and his relationship with Marcus turns from something that he is reluctant to uphold into something which he genuinely enjoys. This change from the unwilling older brother figure into the father Marcus never truly had is something that has a profound effect on not only Marcus, but also Will, as he finally finds a purpose to his life, even though it has sprung upon him so unwittingly.

Personally, I am impressed with the way Will becomes a much more likeable and humane figure towards the end of the book, while still maintaining the image he has worked so hard to achieve, and I think that, ignoring the idea of making a good story, if he had managed to find this balance before in his life, then he would have achieved much more satisfaction and self-worth from his life.

The second student is writing in response to a question on *Never Let Me Go* by Kazuo Ishiguro, which is a novel set some time in the future, and tells the story of a group of young people who, it turns out, have been cloned, or specifically bred, in order to be used for medical purposes. The task here is:

Of the three central characters, Kathy, Tommy and Ruth, with whom do you have the most sympathy and why? Show how Kazuo Ishiguro's presentation of your chosen character creates sympathy for him or her.

Example 2

Of the three central characters, I have the most sympathy with Tommy. He endures a lot of suffering in the book. When he's young, he has temper problems and isn't accepted into the group because of his lack of creativity. Everybody laughs at him and no one respects him at the beginning of the book. Eventually people pick on him just because they like to see him lose his temper. This is shown in the bit where the students are talking about Tommy saying that he isn't creative and that they wished he was taken away by the guardians. This shows that he is an outcast of the friendship groups. Kazuo Ishiguro first shows him as a shy child who is afraid of being found not to be creative; this creates sympathy from the reader because at some point in everyone's lives they have experienced difficulties in doing something and so they can easily put themselves in Tommy's shoes. When Kathy helps him to become accepted he finally has a happier life with her as his best friend. But then Ruth, being a control freak as always, steals him away. She mistreats all her previous friends who were at Hailsham because she wants to fit in to The Cottages. When he's in a relationship with Ruth, she uses him to appear older at the expense of Kathy. She doesn't treat him very well and sleeps around with other people when she is in a relationship with Tommy. I have less sympathy with Ruth because at times she isn't a very nice person. She tells one of Kathy's secrets, when Kathy had trusted her completely. She is a bit domineering in many stages of the book. She decides who is included and excluded from their friendship group. She also forces Marge K to look at the woods, which is a terrifying experience for Marge. When Ruth and Kathy are playing horses, Ruth dictates to Kathy how to play with them. She always likes to be the leader of the group, which makes me think of her as rather bossy.

I have a considerable amount of sympathy with Kathy, but I don't think she has suffered as much as Tommy. Ruth has caused her a considerable amount of hurt over their years together, but Kathy is more included socially than Tommy, because for most of her life she was best friends with Ruth. Secondly, as Kathy is the narrator, it is easy to empathise with her as you can know her thoughts. For instance, when Kathy is looking through the porn mags for her clone parent you can see how upset she is because she and all her friends are cloned from the dregs of society. However, despite the reader's increased empathy towards Kathy, Tommy's suffering throughout life is evident.

GradeStudio

How to go up the grades

Although both responses are focused and show knowledge of the novels, Example 1 is perceptive in its evaluation of the chosen character, and is more developed and considered. It would receive a mark representing A*. Example 2 shows a lot of empathy and awareness, but the points made are not developed in so much detail, and there is not as much specific reference to the events of the novel. However, the thoughtfulness of the response would merit a mark representing grade B.

Putting it into practice

Look closely at the two examples of student responses and write down three reasons why Example 1 achieves the better mark.

Now, look at your response about your most/least sympathetic character, written for Activity 2 page 83. How would you rate what you wrote, comparing it with the levels of response for Examples 1 and 2?

My learning objectives ▼

● to develop confidence in responding to prose essay questions by learning how to write about themes and text specific questions in prose texts

Writing about themes and text specific questions in your prose texts

In the exam you may be asked to write about the themes in one of your set prose texts, and how the author communicates them to the reader.

A theme is an idea or message that the writer may be conveying. You may find the same theme in poetry, novels, or plays. Examples of themes include:

▶ growing up

▶ loneliness

▶ ambition

▶ power

▶ prejudice.

The following activity will help you think about themes and the way they may be presented in your prose text.

Activity 1

1 Working either on your own or in a small group, write down as many themes in your set prose text as you can think of.

2 Then, taking one theme at a time, complete the following (if you are working in a group, discuss and agree your ideas first):
  • the first time in the text when you, as a reader, become aware of the theme (it may even be indicated in the title)
  • how your chosen theme is shown through characters and relationships – choose specific incidents where you think the theme is particularly obvious
  • how your chosen theme is shown through events that happen throughout the story
  • how your chosen theme is important in the text as a whole
  • any occasions where your theme may be reflected in the way the text is written (its use of language, imagery, or the way it is structured).

Text-specific questions on themes

In the exam you may be asked a question that is very specific to your set text, such as the effectiveness of its ending, the significance of its title, or how one particular part is important to the novel/story as a whole. Therefore you need to be prepared to think carefully and organise your ideas quickly.

In the work you have done so far on your text, you will have already covered much of the ground necessary for this, as you have decided on key points throughout the text, discussed characters and relationships, noted important themes and considered the way the writer has written the text, through the use of language and the way it is structured or organised.

You may be asked a question in which the focus is on one or more locations or events in the story. The following activity will help you get this clear in your mind.

Activity 2

1 Working in a small group, create a 'map' of one of your prose texts, clearly labelling different places where events take place.

2 For each place you have identified, add the following details:
   - summarise the main events that take place there
   - list the characters involved in each place
   - write down the themes of the text that are highlighted at each place (if relevant)
   - make a note of the importance of each place to the text as a whole (for example, it may represent a turning point in the development of a character, or in the development of the plot)
   - choose a key quotation to sum up each place.

3 Choose one of the following questions that you think would be suitable for writing about one of your prose texts.
   - How is … [choose an important event in the story here] important to the novel [or a character's life] as a whole?
   - Why do you think … chose to call the text …?
   - To what extent do you find … an effective title for this book?
   - Show how … creates a sense of place in …
   - Which place is the most important in … in your opinion?

4 Make notes or a plan of how you could respond to your chosen question. You will need to decide what method of note-making or planning suits you best. You need to cover these areas:
   - a strong introduction, with clear focus on the question, and establishing your 'take' on the question
   - key areas of the text, from *throughout* the story, that illustrate the points you want to make
   - thoughtful discussion of characters and relationships, with reference to the points you want to make
   - something about the way the text is written – its use of language/symbolism/imagery/structure
   - a strong conclusion to sum up what you have said.

GradeStudio
Examiner tips

In the exam you will improve your answer if you:
- avoid the trap of just telling the story, or re-writing a response to a different question you've completed earlier
- keep a clear focus on the question throughout your response – you should be able to go through what you have written and underline a clear point that refers to the question at least once in every paragraph by using words from the question
- cover the whole of the text – sometimes students focus too much on just one part. You need to show how the text all fits together.

Maya Angelou

These are extracts from a range of responses to text-specific questions. As you read them, check to what extent they:

▶ focus on the question (a useful way to check is to ask yourself 'If the question was not printed here, would I be able to tell what it is?')

▶ refer to specific details in the text.

The first example is an extract from a response to the following question:

In *I Know Why the Caged Bird Sings*, Maya Angelou creates a strong sense of place. With reference to one or two of the places where Maya lived, show how she creates this strong sense of place.

Example 1

Maya Angelou creates a strong sense of place. Two particular places where she does this are Stamps, and San Francisco. In Stamps, Maya seems more relaxed and at home part of the time. In comparison to everywhere else, Stamps is a 'lazy town' and 'much quieter'. Maya, however, seems to create a large sense of belonging and place here. For example, at the Store, Angelou creates a great sense of important community, which makes Maya feel welcome. This is created by using soft images, such as 'the dusky light filtered through the Store, resting on the shelves'. This makes it seem homely, where she belongs. Also, Maya talks about her favourite things such as pineapple, which is in the store. A sense of nostalgia appears occasionally through the older Angelou writing as the younger Maya/Angelou. Furthermore, Maya talks about the community who are brought together at the store, such as the cotton pickers and one of her role models, Mrs Flowers. Also, Angelou creates a place using the Church community, bringing the black community of Stamps together. Maya seems to enjoy it thoroughly and also take scenes from the church services through her life, such as the day when one of the "sisters" started to shout, "Preach it!" and she and Bailey could not control themselves, it portrays the sense of unity and carefree belonging.

Moreover, Angelou uses the sense of the unity of the black community, to create a strong sense of place at the graduation. Even though they could not express their unity in front of the white people, they kept together and waited until they could. This creates a strong sense of place for Maya as she is involved in a large, together, and unified community that stuck together.

San Francisco is another place where Angelou creates a sense of place. For the most part it is because of Mother Dear and the rest of the Baxter family, because they live there and Maya needs to connect with them. However, Angelou creates a sense of unfamiliarity that Maya doesn't agree with. Maya sees it as "a holiday in a foreign place" and that it's too modern, and alien. This, however, contributes to the sense of place created as Maya learns to adapt. Angelou creates the sense of place and belonging with Mother Dear as she connects with Maya, through the process of being modern and more like a friend than a responsible parent.

Examiner comment

The first part of this extract is a very strong and focused opening to the response. The question is kept clearly in sight throughout, and it is supported with detailed reference to the text. There is also an evident appreciation of stylistic features, such as the comment, 'This is created by using soft images', which is then supported by a relevant example.

The second part of the extract shows similar qualities: the focus on the question is being maintained (remember you should keep referring to the question throughout your response), and discussion of relevant detail is thoughtful.

The second example is written in response to:

How is the trial of Tom Robinson important to the novel, *To Kill a Mockingbird*, as a whole?

Example 2

The trial of Tom Robinson takes up the main part of the book. It is very important because of the cultural issues in Maycomb. Tom Robinson is a black person in the book and he is innocent. This is what makes the trial so important.

Everyone from all over Maycomb came to see this trial in their best clothing. This is another indication that this is an important part of the book.

Tom Robinson has been charged because a white woman called Mayella Ewell says she was raped by Tom Robinson. Because of racial issues in the County Tom Robinson is already at a disadvantage because he is black.

We know that the Ewells hate black people because when Atticus was walking out of Tom Robinson's house Mr Ewell was outside with his children and was about to attack them because Atticus was the lawyer for Tom Robinson. When Atticus went to get in his car Mr Ewell said 'Nigger Lover' to Atticus indicating that Atticus is in the wrong. This is where we found out about Ewell's way of living.

Jem and Scout also went to the hearing when their Dad, Atticus told them to specially stay at home. When they got into the court room it was packed to the rim. So they went upstairs to the balcony where all the black members of the county were. This showed great courage because these children were the only white people sat in the balcony. To me this shows that the children believe that equality is an important issue. But I also feel that the answer to this may be that the children do not quite understand what is happening.

As the trial continues Atticus makes it more and more obvious that Mayella Ewell is lying but in everyone else's eyes the white people of the community still choose to believe her.

Therefore as the jury were all white people they found Tom Robinson guilty of the charge against him. Atticus was lost for words because everyone knew that Mayella Ewell was lying but because of the simple fact that Tom Robinson was black he was found guilty, this was one of the ways that white people got rid of the black people in their county because they didn't want them there.

The result of this disaster was that Tom Robinson tried to escape but was shot whilst trying.

At the end of the novel Bob Ewell tries to get revenge on Atticus by attempting to kill his children Jem and Scout but Boo Radley was there and killed him. This shows Bob Ewell's true colours.

Examiner comment

Although this response starts well, with clear focus on the question, and there are references made to the key events of the trial throughout, it would be improved if each of these references were linked back to the point about importance. As it is, there is a tendency to 'tell the story' without any sustained discussion, and it all reads a bit disjointedly.

The final example has been written in response to the following question:

The title 'Of Mice and Men' refers to how plans and dreams often go wrong. To what extent do you find it an effective title for the novel?

Example 3

The title 'Of Mice and Men' is adapted from the poem 'To a Mouse' by Robert Burns. Within the poem were the words 'The best laid plans o' mice and men gang aft agley', which loosely means dreams often go wrong. The title of the novel is effective because it is universal because everyone, from a mouse to a man, can have their dreams shattered.

Possibly one of the most explicit and integral themes in the novel is the theme of dreams. Almost every character within the novel has a dream. However their nature and effect is very different for each, for example 'I coulda been in the pictures', shows how Curley's wife's dream was to be in films which could be seen as quite materialistic or it could simply be a step into achieving her true dream of companionship and her longing for affection. However we can also see each character's dream of owning their own ranch being opposed by their lack of money and therefore being locked within the life of an itinerant ranch worker.

We can also see how many characters' dreams are rivalled by the abundance of prejudices present, 'The boss gives the stable buck hell...he's a nigger.' This could be Steinbeck telling us that it is other people who prevent us from achieving our dreams because of the way we are to each other. It could also be seen as a way in which Steinbeck is trying to emphasise how important companionship is as it can lead to the acquisition of a dream with the help of others, while on the other hand, prejudice such as that shown to Crooks may prevent the achievement of dreams.

Steinbeck creates a sense of hopelessness in the novel in the way that he places all the characters in a continuous cycle from which they will most likely never escape. For example, when George says 'If you get in any trouble come back here..' and Crooks rubbing linament on his back at the beginning and end of section four. This whole idea could show how each character's dream will go wrong because of the way they are to each other. Nobody in the novel shows any level of trust towards another character except George and Lennie. This causes the characters to remain alone because a meaningful relationship cannot be present without trust.

However, there is some hope present within the novel within the relationship of George and Lennie. 'Le's get that place now....sure, right now.' Even though George eventually is the one to end Lennie's life he does it in a way that allows Lennie to die happily in the knowledge that his dream is going to come true. This creates a feeling of tragic irony because only in death, it would seem, can someone come close to achieving their dream.

The same is also true for Curley's wife, "She was in death as she wanted to be in life.....she was very pretty and simple."

I think the title 'Of Mice and Men' is very appropriate because it tries to instill the idea of equality in that no-one can guarantee that they are going to achieve their dream because it very rarely happens for anyone, however simplistic the dream may be.

Examiner comment

This is an assured response, as not only is there clear focus on the question in the first paragraph, but there is also evidence of overview and evaluation right from the start, backed up with very specific reference to key details from the text. Notice how the key point about dreams is referred to throughout – this is the key to a good response.

GradeStudio

How to go up the grades

All three of the responses have strong points: they all focus from the start on the different questions asked, and make references to details from the relevant texts. Example 3 combines the two (i.e. focus and detail) with the most success, although Example 1 is promising, too. Example 2 would benefit from more reference to the question.

Putting it into practice

Choose one of the key themes you have identified, and develop the notes you made in the previous activity into a full essay response to a question, such as:

How does ... present the theme of ... in the novel?
(a typical Higher tier question)

or

Write about the theme of ... in the novel. You may, if you wish, focus on one or two key incidents where ... is important.
(a typical Foundation tier question)

or

How is the theme of ... important in the novel as a whole?
(which, for the Foundation tier, would have bullet points directing you to key parts of the novel or text)

GradeStudio

Examiner tips

In the exam you will improve your answer if you:
- have a strong opening, in which you focus on the theme you are writing about
- keep your focus on the key theme throughout (aim to refer to it in at least every paragraph)
- remember to use your knowledge of the whole novel – reference to key events at different stages of the novel will be helpful here
- show how important characters in the novel highlight the theme
- have a strong conclusion, summing up what you have said in your essay.

Peer/Self-assessment

Now look at your written response to an essay question focusing on themes. How does it compare with the work of the three students on pages 88–90?

You could carry out the steps below on your own work, or swap with a partner, looking at each other's written responses.

- Annotate the response in the same way as the examiner annotated the three students' responses.
- Now try to grade the answer, using the mark scheme in 'Moving up the grades' on page 137.
- Write down three things that would improve the quality of the response.
- Looking at your own work, decide which skills you have developed and used successfully in this response.
- Which skills do you need to develop further?
- Plan how you will achieve the improvements that have been identified as appropriate to your own work.

GradeStudio

Getting the grade!

Read the following student responses to a theme-based question on *Chanda's Secrets* by Allan Stratton. The novel is about the impact of AIDS on a sub-Saharan African family, particularly on the central character, Chanda, the teenage daughter. Read the responses together with the examiner's comments.

The students are writing in response to this question:
How are rumours and superstitions important to the novel as whole?

B grade answer

Student 1

Rumours and superstition are important to this novel. The book relies upon Chanda being naive to the truth and being unaware of the severity of HIV/AIDS. Because of this, Chanda is shocked and confused whenever she hears rumours about the illness and never quite believes that her family could be that 'dirty'. This naivety plays a vital role in the development of Chanda's character and the rumours and superstitions are what trigger the changes.

> Strong opening – clear focus and overview

At the beginning of the book Chanda's sister Sara dies because she has AIDS, but Chanda believes that her sister just died of a bad fever, despite the rumours that have rocked her village. Chanda is also aware that many people are dying in Africa, saying when she goes to the funeral there were 'eight fresh graves', but, although she knows about AIDS, she shuts out the idea that it could happen to anyone close to her.

> Focus on events and detail from the beginning of the novel

Shortly after the death of her sister, her mother's husband (Sara's father) falls ill and dies too. Obviously people begin to wonder how he died, especially since his daughter has just died. However, Chanda insists that, since Jonah was a heavy drinker, he died of alcohol poisoning, despite him becoming very thin and weak. The village then buzzes with rumours of HIV and Chanda's next door neighbour, Mrs. Tafa, a nosy and opinionated woman, even distances herself from the family, not wanting to be associated with a 'dirty family'. Chanda is very confused about this, but starts to wonder whether some rumours are true. This all happens just as Chanda's mum falls ill.

> Detail

> Discussion of character

> Reference to key events – but could develop further

This is a real turn around moment for Chanda because she now has to open her eyes and realise what is going on. Although Chanda is still adamant about ignoring the really horrible rumours, she does realise she needs to mature and accept the reality. This growth then allows her to help her prostitute friend, who has all the village talking. Chanda decides to ignore the village and help her friend, even though this means everyone deserting her. Rumours continue to spread when her mum runs away but Chanda's new found maturity means she convinces the village to accept the illness and people's attitudes towards the family. The rumours are quashed once Chanda faces the truth, and even though her mother dies, Chanda finds herself better able to cope with her life.

> Valid point – but lacks detailed support

> Underdeveloped reference

> Rather rushed conclusion, skimming over important events

Examiner comment

This response starts strongly, with a clear overview, and deals in some detail with events in the first part of the novel. Later events are rather skimmed over, but the thoughtfulness in this response would help it get a mark representing grade B.

Student 2

Rumours and superstitions are important to the novel because Chanda is unaware of the disease that is spreading as she thinks it is a mere superstition. Also, the rumours about AIDS are that it is a 'dirty' disease and people do not want to be associated with AIDS or people who have the disease.

> Clear focus on question

Chanda is very naive, and when rumours spread that people she knows have AIDS, she denies them. However, Chanda denies these rumours, purely because she genuinely does not believe that they have had AIDS. Although Chanda's sister has died, she thinks it cannot be AIDS related because her sister was still an infant. However, because Chanda's mother had AIDS when she was pregnant, her sister became infected. This is very important in the novel because Chanda gradually realises the truth about AIDS. Chanda's neighbour, Mrs.Tafa, spreads rumours about the disease and tries to gain information about Chanda's mother when she falls ill. This is important because everybody is told by her that the whole family is ill with AIDS and everybody becomes very cautious of the family.

> Reference to background/ discussion of character

> Apt reference – could be more specific

Chanda's friend Esther is a prostitute, but Chanda refuses to accept this. She believes that she merely has her photograph taken with tourists. However, when Esther falls ill, and Chanda finds out that it is AIDS, she sees the reality of what her friend does to earn money. When Chanda discovers the truth, the reality of her illness becomes clear. Chanda gradually begins to realise the truth of the disease her family and friend had. The rumours and superstitions are important to the novel in this sense, because she knows they were all true and she was living believing lies.

> Reference

> Discussion

> Rather general conclusion

Examiner comment

Student 2's response starts well, and goes on to discuss characters and relationships. However, it does not show detailed knowledge of the whole novel, and the examiner would wonder if the student had actually read it all. Because of this, Student 2's response would get a mark representing a low C.

How to go up the grades

Both these responses start with a clear focus on the question, although Student 1 gets off to a better start, by including some discussion of the key character in the first paragraph. Student 1 develops points in more detail – Student 2 clearly knows the story, and details about some of the important characters, but does not develop these points sufficiently. Both responses would have benefitted from the inclusion of key events from *throughout* the novel. This shows how helpful it is to have key references from the whole novel in your mind, as part of your preparation. You will then be able to use these key references in whichever question you choose to answer in the exam. Student 1's response would get a mark representing a low B, as it is thoughtful and focused, but could be more detailed and specific in its references. Student 2's response would get a mark representing a low C. To get a higher mark there would have to be more reference to the details of the story to support the points made about rumours and superstitions.

Putting it into practice

Now look at the practice response to the question you devised, based on a key theme in your prose text. How would you rate what you wrote, comparing it with the levels of response for Student 1 and Student 2? What, if anything, would you have to do to improve your response to theme-based questions?

3 Drama

Contemporary and literary heritage

You will study and answer questions on **one** drama text in the examination.

In **Unit 2** you will answer questions **either** on **one** of the following literary heritage drama texts:

- *Othello* by William Shakespeare
- *Much Ado About Nothing* by William Shakespeare
- *An Inspector Calls* by J.B. Priestley
- *Hobson's Choice* by Harold Brighouse
- *A Taste of Honey* by Shelagh Delaney

or on **one** of the following contemporary drama texts:

- *The History Boys* by Alan Bennett
- *Blood Brothers* by Willy Russell
- *A View From the Bridge* by Arthur Miller
- *Be My Baby* by Amanda Whittington
- *My Mother Said I Never Should* by Charlotte Keatley

For all these drama texts, the pattern of questions will be the same, for both Foundation and Higher tiers.

- First, you will answer a single question, basing your response on a close reading of an **extract** from the play, which is printed on the exam paper. This should take you about **20 minutes**, including reading time.
- Then you will choose from one of two essay titles, where you will show your knowledge of the **whole text**. This should take you about **40 minutes**, including thinking, planning, and checking time.

These are the assessment criteria that you will be assessed against.

Assessment Objectives:

A01 Respond to texts critically and imaginatively; select and evaluate relevant textual detail to illustrate and support interpretations.

A02 Explain how language, structure and form contribute to writers' presentation of ideas, themes and settings.

3.1 Drama extract questions

The pattern of questions will be similar for all drama texts and also similar to those you saw in the prose section. The following questions are typical of the questions you are likely to see in your exam. Note that questions tend to focus on either **characters**, or on **mood and atmosphere** (or **thoughts and feelings** on the Foundation tier).

Higher tier questions

On the Higher tier you will find questions such as:

▶ Look closely at how … and … speak and behave here. What does it reveal about their relationship?

▶ Look closely at how … and … speak and behave here. What impressions would an audience receive of their characters?

▶ Look closely at how … speaks and behaves here. How may it affect an audience's feelings towards him/her?

▶ Look closely at how … speaks and behaves here. What does it reveal about his/her character?

▶ Look closely at how … speaks and behaves here. What does it reveal about his/her feelings?

▶ Look closely at how … and … speak and behave here. How does it create mood and atmosphere for an audience?

▶ With close reference to the extract, show how the playwright creates mood and atmosphere for an audience here.

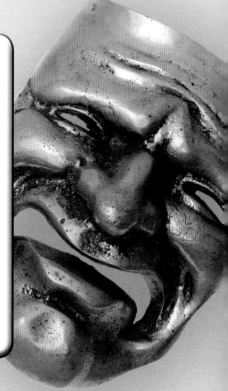

Foundation tier questions

On the Foundation tier you will find questions such as:

▶ What do you think of the way … speaks and behaves here? Give reasons for what you say and remember to support your answer with words and phrases from the extract.
▶ What do you think of the way … and … speak and behave here? Remember to support your answer with words and phrases from the text.
▶ What are your thoughts and feelings as you read this extract? Give reasons for what you say, and remember to support your answer with words and phrases from the text.
▶ What are your thoughts and feelings about the relationship between … and … as you read this extract? Remember to support your answer with words and phrases from the extract.

GradeStudio

Examiner tips

In the exam you will improve your answer if you:

● bear in mind that **plays are intended to be performed for an audience**, and when you read a play, or an extract from it, you are the audience at that time
● look closely at how the characters speak and behave – which means reading the **stage directions** as closely as you read the dialogue
● have a clear focus on the question asked throughout your response
● select key details from throughout the extract, being as thorough as you can, while making sure everything you select is relevant to the question
● link the points you select and comment on to the overview (your 'take' on the question)
● clearly refer to the question – decide what you think and sum up your response in a sentence or two, and then refer to the question throughout your response
● look carefully at the ending of the extract – there's a reason why it ends where it does!

My learning objectives ▼

- to develop confidence in responding to drama extract questions by learning how to build skills in the close reading of stage directions

Stage directions

Close reading of the stage directions can make a real difference to the grade you receive in the exam, so use them as much as you can. If you are studying Shakespeare as your set drama text, you will notice that there are few stage directions. That's because they tend to be embedded in the dialogue. Shakespeare usually makes it clear how his characters should speak and behave (and creates mood and atmosphere) through the way he uses language in his characters' lines, so you need to look particularly closely at the dialogue for clues about this.

Read the following extract from *An Inspector Calls*, by J.B. Priestley. The events of the play take place over one evening in 1912, in the home of the Birling family, whose life is shattered by the arrival of the mysterious, and, possibly, supernatural, Inspector Goole, who calls with the news of the death by suicide of a young pregnant woman called Eva Smith, and, sometimes, Daisy Renton.

This extract is from near the end of the play. Inspector Goole has systematically made each member of the rich and powerful Birling family (Mr. and Mrs. Birling, their children Eric and Sheila, and Sheila's fiance, Gerald Croft) admit their connection with Eva Smith. At this point in the play, the Inspector has done his work, and is about to end his visit to the Birlings.

INSPECTOR: *(cutting in)* And my trouble is – that I haven't much time. You'll be able to divide the responsibility between you when I've gone. *(To ERIC.)* Just one last question, that's all. The girl discovered that this money you were giving her was stolen, didn't she?

ERIC: *(miserably)* Yes. That was the worst of all. She wouldn't take any more, and she didn't want to see me again. *(Suddenly startled tone.)* Here, but how did you know that? Did she tell you?

INSPECTOR: No. She told me nothing. I never spoke to her.

SHEILA: She told mother.

MRS B.: *(alarmed)* Sheila!

SHEILA: Well, he has to know.

ERIC: *(to MRS BIRLING)* She told you? Did she come here – but then she couldn't have done, she didn't even know I lived here. What happened?

MRS BIRLING, *distressed, shakes her head but does not reply.*

Come on, don't just look like that. Tell me – tell me – what happened?

INSPECTOR: *(with calm authority)* I'll tell you. She went to your mother's committee for help, after she'd done with you. Your mother refused that help.

ERIC: *(nearly at breaking point)* Then – you killed her. She came to you to protect me – and you turned her away – yes, and you killed her – and the child she'd have had too – my child – your own grandchild – you killed them both – damn you, damn you –

MRS B.: *(very distressed now)* No – Eric – please – I didn't know – I didn't understand –

ERIC: *(almost threatening her)* You don't understand anything. You never did. You never even tried – you –

SHEILA: *(frightened)* Eric, don't – don't –

BIRLING: *(furious, intervening)* Why, you hysterical young fool – get back – or I'll –

INSPECTOR: *(taking charge, masterfully)* Stop! *They are suddenly quiet, staring at him.* And be quiet for a moment and listen to me. I don't need to know any more. Neither do you. This girl killed herself – and died a horrible death. But each of you helped to kill her. Remember that. Never forget it. *(He looks from one to the other of them carefully.)* But then I don't think you ever will.

The following activity will help you understand the significance of stage directions in any extract from a play.

Activity 1

1 Working on your own, or in a small group, make a list of all the stage directions (the bits written in italics), and then, by each stage direction, make a note of what it tells the audience (i.e. you!) about what's going on, as in the following:

Stage direction	Comment
cutting in	the Inspector is getting impatient
miserably	Eric's feeling sorry for himself? Or guilty?
suddenly startled tone	realises his secret's out
alarmed	Mrs. B. shocked at Sheila letting Eric know what's been going on

2 Now, read the dialogue ignoring the stage directions.

3 Compare the two versions, with and without stage directions. What differences do you notice in the understanding an audience would have of what's going on, and what the mood and atmosphere is?

4 Next, choose an extract from your set drama text (a page to a page and a half should be fine), and do the same exercise, isolating the stage directions from the dialogue. If your set play is Shakespeare, select any features, stage directions, or words and phrases, that tell the actors how to behave.

5 Think about the effect the stage directions have had on your interpretation of your chosen extract.

Remember what you did, Mrs Birling. You turned her away when she most needed help. You refused her even the pitiable little bit of organised charity you had in your power to grant her. Remember what you did –

ERIC: *(unhappily)* My God – I'm not likely to forget.

INSPECTOR: Just used her for the end of a stupid drunken evening, as if she was an animal, a thing, not a person. No, you won't forget. *(He looks at SHEILA.)*

SHEILA: *(bitterly)* I know. I had her turned out of a job. I started it.

INSPECTOR: You helped – but didn't start it. *(Rather savagely, to BIRLING.)* You started it. She wanted twenty-five shillings a week instead of twenty-two and sixpence. You made her pay a heavy price for that. And now she'll make you pay a heavier price still.

BIRLING: *(unhappily)* Look, Inspector – I'd give thousands – yes, thousands –

INSPECTOR: You're offering the money at the wrong time, Mr Birling. *(He makes a move as if concluding the session, possibly shutting up notebook, etc. Then surveys them sardonically.)* No, I don't think any of you will forget. Nor that young man, Croft, though he at least had some affection for her and made her happy for a time. Well, Eva Smith's gone. You can't do her any more harm. And you can't do her any good now, either. You can't even say 'I'm sorry, Eva Smith'.

SHEILA: *(who is crying quietly)* That's the worst of it.

INSPECTOR: But just remember this. One Eva Smith has gone – but there are millions and millions and millions of Eva Smiths and John Smiths still left with us, with their lives, their hopes and fears, their suffering and chance of happiness, all intertwined with our lives, and what we think and say and do. We don't live alone. We are members of one body. We are responsible for each other. And I tell you that the time will soon come when, if men will not learn that lesson, then they will be taught it in fire and blood and anguish. Good night.

He walks straight out, leaving them staring, subdued and wondering.

GradeStudio

Examiner tips

Remember to use the stage directions as well as the dialogue to support your answer.

Read the following extract from *Hobson's Choice*. This is a play about the owner (the Hobson of the title) of a shoe shop in Salford, Lancashire, in the late 19th century. He has three daughters, Maggie, Vickey and Alice. When Maggie realises that her father thinks she will always be there for him, as she will never marry, she takes matters into her own hands, and marries Willie Mossop, her father's bootmaker. They set up a successful business, and Maggie also helps Vickey and Alice to marry and escape their father. When Hobson fails to cope, Maggie and Willie return, to set up a partnership. This extract shows their return, near the end of the play.

Hobson's Choice

WILLIE: Now, then, Maggie, go and bring your father down and be sharp. I'm busy at my shop, so what they are at his. (*MAGGIE takes Willie's hat off and puts it on the settee, then exits*) It's been a good business in its day, too, has Hobson's.

ALICE: What on earth do you mean? It's a good business still.

WILLIE: You try to sell it, and you'd learn. Stock and goodwill 'ud fetch about two hundred.

VICKEY: Don't talk so foolish, Will. Two hundred for a business like father's!

WILLIE: Two hundred as it is. Not as it was in our time, Vickey.

ALICE: Do you mean to tell me father isn't rich?

WILLIE: If you'd not married into the law you'd know what they think of your father today in trading circles. Vickey ought to know. Her husband's in trade.

VICKEY (*indignantly*): My Fred in trade!

WILLIE: Isn't he?

VICKEY: He's in the wholesale. That's business, not trade. And the value of father's shop is no affair of yours, Will Mossop.

WILLIE: Now I thought maybe it was. If Maggie and me are coming here.

VICKEY: You're coming to look after father.

WILLIE: Maggie can do that with one hand tied behind her back. I'll look after the business.

ALICE: You'll do what's arranged for you.

WILLIE: I'll do the arranging, Alice. If we come here, we come here on my terms.

VICKEY: They'll be fair terms.

WILLIE: I'll see they're fair to me and Maggie.

ALICE: Will Mossop, do you know who you're talking to?

WILLIE (*turning*): Aye. My wife's young sisters. Times have changed a bit since you used to order me about this shop, haven't they, Alice?

ALICE: Yes. I'm Mrs Albert Prosser now.

WILLIE: So you are, to outsiders. And you'd be surprised the number of people that call me Mr Mossop now. We do get on in the world, don't we?

ALICE moves up stage

VICKEY: Some folks get on too fast.

WILLIE: It's a matter of opinion. I know Maggie and me gave both of you a big leg up when we arranged your marriage portions, but I dunno that we're grudging you the sudden lift you got.

Enter HOBSON and MAGGIE

WILLIE: Good morning, father. I'm sorry to hear you're not so well.

HOBSON: I'm a changed man, Will. (*He comes down and sits on the armchair*)

WILLIE: There used to be room for improvement.

HOBSON: What! (*He starts up*)

MAGGIE: Sit down, father.

WILLIE: Aye. Don't let us be too long about this. You've kept me waiting now a good while and my time's valuable. I'm busy at my shop.

HOBSON: Is your shop more important than my life?

WILLIE: That's a bit like asking if a pound of tea weighs heavier than a pound of lead. I'm worrited about your life because it worrits Maggie, but I'm none worrited that bad I'll see my business suffer for the sake of you.

HOBSON: This isn't what I've a right to expect from you, Will.

WILLIE: You've no right to expect I care whether you sink or swim.

MAGGIE: Will!

WILLIE: What's to do? You told me to take a high hand, didn't you?

MAGGIE sits down

Read the following openings to responses to this extract from *Hobson's Choice*. The students are writing in response to the question:

Look closely at how Willie speaks and behaves here. What does it reveal to an audience about him?

In your opinion, which example gives the best overview of the extract, and by so doing creates a good basis for the rest of the answer?

Example 1

The way Willie speaks and behaves here reveals to the audience many different things, but the main thing that is revealed is the way he has changed from previously being a quiet, gentle, timid, lower-class shoemaker to now being a prosperous, hard, middle class businessman. 'I'm busy at my shop' instantly tells the audience three things: Willie owns a shop, his shop is busy and he is not going to let 'petty' matters interfere with the prosperity of his business. He uses quite precise language and complex words to put across his sharp, literal statements: 'Stock and goodwill 'ud fetch about two hundred' shows his unproud, truthful statements which hit Alice and Vickey's pride hard. Willie does not attempt to submit to his sister-in-laws' pride; he tells them the stark truth and will not regard them as any higher class than he is. This is shown when he refers to Vickey: 'Vickey ought to know. Her husband's in trade.'

Example 2

I think the audience would react very well to this part of the play as they see a totally different Willie Mossop: a stronger, more confident man. I think that Willie is speaking as if he is a traditional middle/upper-class man of that time. He speaks as if he is important: 'Now, then, Maggie, go and bring your father ... I'm busy at my shop.' Here Willie is speaking as if he is the boss and is in charge of Maggie and the business. 'You try to sell it, and you'd learn.' Here Will is showing that he is clever and understands the business trade. 'I'll do the arranging, Alice. If we come here, we come here on my terms.' Again Willie is showing Alice and Vickey that he is in charge and that Maggie follows his orders. I think the audience would be greatly amused by Willie as he delivers some really funny and clever lines: 'You've no right to expect I care whether you sink or swim.' This is in response to Hobson asking if he cares what becomes of him. His reply is so out of character that even Maggie is shocked.

Example 3

We immediately see that Will has become assertive. He tells Maggie to 'go and bring your father down and be sharp', which shows that Will has learnt to take control of situations. He also says that he will 'do the arranging', which shows he is now prepared to make decisions about his life rather than just letting other people do it for him. Will has also become very knowledgeable and worldly: 'It's been a good business in its day, too, has Hobson's.' This shows that he understands the changes in Hobson's and the reasons for the changes. He also appears to take pride in his understanding of business: 'You try to sell it, and you'd learn', which shows he realises that his own understanding is above that of Alice and Vickey. Will has become very confident in his own abilities. He says 'I'll look after the business' which shows he knows he is capable of running a business well. Will is proud of what he has achieved. He refers to his shoe shop as 'my shop' and says his 'time's valuable', which shows he is proud and now values himself because of the successful life he has made for himself and Maggie. Will has become quite comfortable around Mr Hobson, whom he once feared. He calls him 'father' quite happily, which he once felt uncomfortable doing.

GradeStudio

How to go up the grades

There are positive qualities to all three responses.

Example 1, after a rather general opening, becomes more focused, with some overview, referring to Willie's changed character. It proceeds to work through the extract, selecting and highlighting detail, although these points could be more developed, and there could be more awareness of the audience's response.

Example 2 makes similar points but is rather more engaged with the extract and the focus of the question, with a real awareness of the impact the extract would have on the audience, and clear points about Willie's speech and behaviour. It could be more systematic in approach, however, by tracking through the extract.

Example 3 has a strong, focused start (the reference to 'we' in the first sentence is valid in showing a response as an audience). It goes on to read the extract closely, evaluating Willie's speech and behaviour thoughtfully, and maintaining the overview established from the start. One of the strengths of this response is the close focus on detail to support the overview.

On balance, then, Example 3 is the best, followed by Example 2, then Example 1.

The following activity will give you practice in being specific in your comments on characters.

Activity 3

1 Choose an extract from your set play in which one of the main characters is playing a significant part.

2 Think of as many adjectives as you can to describe your chosen character. List them down the left-hand side of a piece of paper.

3 For each adjective you have chosen, provide evidence from the text to support your choice, in the form of a brief quotation or a direct reference.

4 Now write up your notes in response to a question such as *Look closely at how … speaks and behaves here. What does it reveal of his/her feelings?*
Or, for the Foundation tier, *What do you think of the way … speaks and behaves here? Remember to support your answer with words and phrases from the extract.*

GradeStudio

Examiner tips

In the exam you will improve your answer if you:
- use specific details to show you know the text well
- discuss the behaviour of characters thoughtfully and sensitively
- refer to key themes.

Focusing your response

The following activity will help you focus from the very beginning of your response to a drama text.

Activity 4

1 From the drama text you are studying, select another extract that asks for your response to how a character is speaking and behaving. The extract should be fairly short (about a page or a page and a half).

2 Choose one of the extract questions on pages 96–97 to provide the focus of your question.

3 Now write the first paragraph of your response to the question you have created.

GradeStudio

Examiner tips

You should:
- briefly contextualise the extract (explain how it fits into the story)
- focus on the question right from the start, as well as throughout your response
- use the stage directions as much as the dialogue to support the points you are making.

My learning objectives ▼

- to develop confidence in responding to drama extract questions by learning how to build skills in writing about mood and atmosphere

Writing about mood and atmosphere

The following activity will help you to write a response to a mood and atmosphere question on your set drama text. (On the Foundation tier this may ask you how you think an audience would respond to the way the characters speak and behave, giving reasons for what you say, and remembering to support your answer with words and phrases from the extract.)

Activity 1

1 Choose an extract from your drama text in which you think there is a strong mood and atmosphere or that you think would have a strong impact on an audience.

2 Then, choose the focus of your response (mood and atmosphere, which is typically found on the Higher tier, or how an audience would respond to the way the characters speak and behave, which is more likely to be found on the Foundation tier).

3 Decide what your point of view is, then select and highlight details that support your point of view.

4 Now, write your response to the question you have created.

You should:

- decide what you want to say before you start to write, so that your response has a clear focus

- remember that you are a valid audience, so think about whether you find the extract exciting, sad, dramatic, romantic, angry, and so on, but it may also be useful to think about how other audiences may respond

- bear in mind that the mood and atmosphere (or an audience's reactions) may change as the extract develops, but you can still show an awareness of that from the start.

Remember to:

- put the extract in context (explain how it fits into the story) and focus on the question asked right from the start, so that you 'hit the ground running'

- select words and phrases (the shorter these quotations the better) to support your point of view, remembering to use the whole of the extract, choosing details from the beginning, the middle, and the end!

- explain how the selected words and phrases support the points you are making (the PEE pattern, as some call it)

- remember to keep an eye on the clock – in the exam you will have to do this sort of activity in 20 minutes, including thinking and planning.

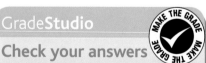

GradeStudio

Check your answers

Look back on your answer.

- Have you started your answer with a clear focus on the question?
- Have you kept focus on the question throughout your answer?
- Have you selected and highlighted detail from throughout the extract?
- Have you remembered to use the stage directions, if there are any, reading them as closely as you read the dialogue between the characters?
- Have you linked your selected details to the points you want to make?

The extract below is from *Be My Baby* by Amanda Whittington. The play is set in a home for young pregnant girls in the 1960s. The extract is from the end of the play, when Mrs Adams, the mother of one of the girls, Mary, comes to take her home after she has had her baby, which she is leaving behind to be adopted. Queenie is one of the other girls in the home.

Be My Baby

Enter MATRON and MRS ADAMS. Exit QUEENIE.

MRS ADAMS: Mary?

MARY: Mother.

MATRON: Nearly done?

MARY: Not quite, Matron.

MRS ADAMS: Nearly done.

MARY: How was your journey?

MRS ADAMS: Rather slow.

MARY: Is Father. . .

MRS ADAMS: Glad to hear your Aunt's on the mend.

MRS ADAMS gets MARY's coat and holds it open for her.

MRS ADAMS: I've spoken to the bank. You start a new job on Monday.

MARY: This Monday?

MRS ADAMS: City centre branch, no less.

MARY: I liked it where I was.

MRS ADAMS: We've been rather busy since you've been away. Father took the opportunity to decorate your room.

MARY: It was a girl, Mother.

MARY puts on her coat.

MRS ADAMS: Button up, Mary.

MARY: I held her.

MRS ADAMS: You don't want to feel the cold.

MARY: I kept her warm 'til morning.

MRS ADAMS: Come along, Mary. You're a big girl, now.

MARY puts the Dansette and records on QUEENIE's bed.

MARY: For Queenie.

MATRON: I'd rather you took it.

MARY: So she doesn't forget.

MRS ADAMS: The taxi's waiting.

MARY: I'm not ready.

MRS ADAMS: Then let me help you.

MARY: No, Mother. I'll follow you down.

MATRON: Shall I show you out?

MARY: She knows the way.

MRS ADAMS: Mary?

MATRON: It's all right. I'll bring her down.

Exit MRS ADAMS.

MATRON: Well?

MARY: Not really.

MATRON: You will be.

MARY: If you say so.

MATRON: It's over, Mary. Time to go home.

MARY hands her teddy bear to MATRON.

MARY: For Lucy. My baby.

MATRON takes the teddy bear. Exit MARY. MATRON holds the teddy bear as 'Be My Baby' plays to blackout.

THE END

Activity 2

Below are examples of two student responses to the question:

With close reference to the extract, show how Amanda Whittington creates mood and atmosphere for an audience here.

Read the student responses together with this checklist of points:

	Student 1	Student 2
Clear focus on the question		
Thorough discussion of the extract		
Relevant reference to the play, in order to put the extract in context		
Selection and highlighting of detail to support the points made		

Which response do you think would get the better mark? Why?

Student 1

Amanda Whittington creates a tense and awkward mood and atmosphere here by having Mary speak very bluntly – when her mum asks 'Mary?', instead of responding politely 'Yes?', she just states 'Mother'. The atmosphere gets tenser when Mrs Adams and Mary give conflicting answers to Matron's question, 'Nearly done?' Mrs Adams interrupts Mary to stop her, making the mood more tense. Mrs Adams then 'gets Mary's coat' and 'holds it open for her' which shows she wants to get rid of her quicker. The atmosphere gets thicker when Mary makes it obvious her new job does not take her interest and she prefers her current one. She tells her mother bluntly, 'It was a girl', but the atmosphere thickens when her mum simply ignores this statement, telling her to 'button up'. This continues when Mary ignores what her mum said, saying 'I held her' and her mother ignores this, saying, 'you don't want to feel the cold.' The awkward atmosphere is created because the majority of the speech is made up of short simple sentences to show that they are treading on egg shells in their speech. Mary is not ready to go and does not want her mum's help which she makes very clear to her. Her mum leaves and Mary has a talk with matron which ends with 'For Lucy. My baby.' bringing the scene to an end very tensely.

Student 2

In the extract the writer tells us what happens when Mary's mother comes to pick her up after she had given her baby away. It starts off very interestingly with 'Mary?' 'Mother.' This one word introduction almost sets up the rest of the conversation – there has been no 'How are you?' or 'How was it?'

The conversation is very matter of fact and sets up the tense mood and atmosphere. This is because Mrs Adams doesn't ask Mary about the emotions of the situation. When Mary says 'It was a girl, Mother' Mrs Adams replies with 'Button up' changing the conversation, swiftly moving on. When Mary talks about how she 'held her…'til morning' her mother reminds her that she is a 'big girl', this shows how the mother really doesn't want to be talking about the baby.

Mary later says 'If you say so' which shows a conflict between her and Matron, which helps set the mood and atmosphere.

GradeStudio

How to go up the grades

Student 1's response starts strongly, with clear focus on the question straightaway, by identifying the mood and atmosphere. This is supported by a clear understanding of the tone of the characters' speech, highlighted through relevant detail. There is evidence of close reading, for example in the reference to 'Mrs Adams interrupts Mary… ' and valid inference from the stage directions. There is some appreciation of style and effect, in the reference to the short simple sentences suggesting how they are 'treading on egg shells', although this could be developed. This response would get a mark representing a clear grade B. To get a higher mark, it would have been helpful to be clearer about the context of the extract (particularly as it is the end of the play) and to have focused more on the ending of the extract, including the closing stage directions.

Student 2 starts by setting the extract in context, but only focuses on the mood and atmosphere, and, therefore, the question, in the second paragraph of the response. There is some selection of detail, and discussion of the characters' speech and behaviour, but this could be much more detailed. This response would get a mark representing grade C/D. To get a higher mark, this response would need to be more thorough, with a closer focus on the question all the way through.

Putting it into practice

Now look at your practice response to your set play. How would you rate what you wrote, comparing it with the levels of response for Students 1 and 2?

Writing about more than one character

The following activity will help you answer questions that ask you to look at the speech and behaviour of more than one character in an extract from a play.

Activity 1

1   Choose an extract from your set play that is a good example of characters interacting with (communicating with or affecting) one another. About a page should be long enough, but make sure it has a clear opening and ending.

2   Choose the focus of your response. Focus on the impressions an audience gains from how the characters speak and behave, which is typically found on the Higher tier, or on your thoughts about the characters' speech and behaviour (supported by words and phrases from the text), which is typically found on the Foundation tier.

3   Write your response to the question you have created, such as *Look closely at how … and … speak and behave here. What impressions would an audience receive of their characters?* Or *What do you think of the way … and … speak and behave here? Give reasons for what you say, and remember to support your answer with words and phrases from the extract.*

Activity 2

In Shakespeare's *Much Ado About Nothing*, Don Pedro, the Prince of Aragon, and his soldiers, including the young officer Claudio, have just returned from war. In this extract, Don Pedro says that he will support Claudio in his courtship of Hero, the daughter of Leonato, the Governor of Messina. However, his idea for doing this, by pretending to be Claudio, seems a bit suspicious!

When you have read it, make notes in answer to one of the following questions (the first is a Foundation question, the second a Higher question):

What do you think of the way Claudio and Don Pedro speak and behave here? Give reasons for what you say, and remember to support your answer with words and phrases from the extract.

Look closely at how Claudio and Don Pedro speak and behave here. What impressions would an audience receive of their characters?

Much Ado About Nothing

CLAUDIO: My liege, your Highness now may do me good.

DON PEDRO: My love is thine to teach. Teach it but how,
And thou shalt see how apt it is to learn
Any hard lesson that may do thee good.

CLAUDIO: Hath Leonato any son, my lord?

DON PEDRO: No child but Hero: she's his only heir.
Dost thou affect her, Claudio?

CLAUDIO: O my lord,
When you went onward on this ended action,
I looked upon her with a soldier's eye,
That liked, but had a rougher task in hand
Than to drive liking to the name of love.
But now I am returned, and that war-thoughts
Have left their places vacant, in their rooms
Come thronging soft and delicate desires,
All prompting me how fair young Hero is,
Saying I liked her ere I went to wars.

DON PEDRO: Thou wilt be like a lover presently,
And tire the hearer with a book of words.
If thou dost love fair Hero, cherish it;
And I will break with her and with her father
And thou shalt have her. Was't not to this end
That thou began'st to twist so fine a story?

CLAUDIO: How sweetly you do minister to love,
That know love's grief by his complexion!
But lest my liking might too sudden seem,
I would have salved it with a longer treatise.

DON PEDRO: What need the bridge much broader
    than the flood?
The fairest grant is the necessity.
Look what will serve is fit. 'Tis once, thou lovest,
And I know we shall have revelling tonight:
I will assume thy part in some disguise,
And tell fair Hero I am Claudio,
And in her bosom I'll unclasp my heart,
And take her hearing prisoner with the force
And strong encounter of my amorous tale.
Then after, to her father will I break:
And the conclusion is, she shall be thine.
In practice let us put it presently.

GradeStudio

Getting the grade!

Here are two students' responses to the task in Activity 2 on page 108. Read the answers together with the examiner's comments.

As you read them, think about the way the students have focused on the question, and selected and highlighted details to support their ideas.

the task in Activity 2 on page 108

C grade answer

Student 1

Clear focus

I think that Claudio is not keen to let on what he is feeling. He asks if Hero's father Leonato has a son. This is so it is not obvious that he likes Hero, but Don Pedro realises and asks Claudio if he does 'affect her'.

Some discussion

Claudio is not too eager to show what he feels now, that he likes Hero, as before he went to war he 'looked upon her with a soldier's eye'. He did not intend to marry her, but for other less proper reasons. Even with this small speech we can tell how Claudio's character has changed. He doesn't just want sex now, he wants a proper relationship. Don Pedro seems convinced by Claudio and says he will make him a 'lover presently'. He promises that he'll persuade Leonato and Hero that Claudio loves Hero, and won't stop until they agree to Hero marrying Claudio.

Aware – but lacks support

Paraphrasing

Claudio is really grateful. He says he'll keep his true feelings hidden for longer until the time is better. But Don Pedro seems shocked by this and believes that if you love someone you should be with them. From this point Don Pedro makes a plan to get Hero for Claudio. I think he is being a good friend to Claudio even though he is making plots.

Aware

Judging characters and relationships

Empathy

I also feel sorry for Hero with all this going on behind her back. Don Pedro and Claudio are acting as if Hero and her father have no choice, although maybe this is the only way Claudio can win Hero. Maybe if he went to see Hero and Leonato himself, Hero's father would not approve of him and not let him marry her. I think that maybe the end will justify the means.

Examiner comment

Student 1 has responded clearly to the extract, and has discussed the characters' behaviour within the context of the extract and the play. However, there is a tendency to comment and explain what is happening without support from the extract. The student shows empathy, begins to discuss the way the characters speak and behave, and is mainly well focused. This response would receive a mark representing grade C.

MOVING UP THE GRADES

How to go up the grades

Student 1 could have achieved a better grade by making closer reference to the words and phrases of the extract, and by developing the points made. Student 2's response is confident, focuses closely on Shakespeare's language, and offers alternative interpretations – all important features of A* candidates' work.

Putting it into practice

Now look at your practice response to the extract you selected from your set play. How would you rate what you wrote, comparing it with the responses of Students 1 and 2?

Student 2

Shakespeare presents a revealing conversation between Don Pedro and his deputy, Claudio. We see Claudio reveal the rekindling of his feelings for Hero. This extract shows us a lot about Don Pedro and Claudio's characters and is the start of the story of Claudio's relationship with Hero.

Although the relationship between Don Pedro and Claudio is prince and deputy, it seems to have become more like student and teacher or father and son, or friends, as is shown by the easy way they talk together.

Despite this, Claudio still shows respect for Don Pedro by using terms such as 'my liege' and 'your Highness'. It is clear also that there is self-interest in Claudio as he says that Don Pedro 'may do me good'. However, this self-interest is driven by his love for Hero which is evident throughout the play. Don Pedro seems to be a fair and caring master and this is shown by his willingness to help Claudio in such statements as 'My love is thine to teach.' Perhaps this is because Don Pedro wants to be a tutor to Claudio, or perhaps it shows the patriarchal society shown throughout the play. Don Pedro is also shown as an incredibly perceptive character as he immediately detects Claudio's feelings for Hero, just from Claudio's seemingly casual question of whether Leonato has a son. When Claudio explains his feelings for Hero the audience may interpret this in different ways. Perhaps Claudio's new 'soft and delicate desires' which replace his 'war-thoughts' show a rashness of character, which is strengthened by his rashness throughout the play, when he is tricked into believing his beloved Hero to be nothing more than 'cunning sin'. Another possible interpretation would be that Claudio's military nature really has changed, and his newfound feelings really show love for Hero. This interpretation is strengthened by Benedick's comments that Claudio now prefers the melodies of the civilian tabor and pipe.

Don Pedro seems to be experienced in romantic matters as he says that Claudio shall be 'like a lover presently' as if he has seen Claudio's actions many a time. There is a sense of disdain in his words when he says that love inspires people to 'tire the hearer with a book of words' and this could suggest Don Pedro has too often seen love pass him by, or maybe he has been hurt too many times. Although Claudio is in love with Hero he seems to proceed cautiously as he thinks it wise to have 'salved' his love 'with a longer treatise', which suggests that Claudio is not so certain, or maybe these true feelings of love are so new to him that he is surprised by their powerful effects on him. Don Pedro uses romantic imagery to express love, describing his feelings as a 'flood', suggesting he may believe that love is ever flowing and washes away all obstacles in its path. Perhaps the way he seems so keen to press Claudio's cause with Hero while Claudio is more cautious suggests that Don Pedro wants to live through his young deputy, or perhaps he sees Claudio's feelings as pure and noble and not something that could be 'salved'.

Overall the pair seem contented with their positions as Claudio easily accepts his master's suggestions and commands, perhaps suggesting a weakness of character or just recognising Don Pedro's dominance, and Don Pedro revels in the romantic advancement of Claudio. An audience may find immaturity in both characters as Claudio seems romantically naive, while Don Pedro has a boyish delight in manipulating the situation. The characters however are portrayed as generally likeable within this scene as Claudio's feelings do seem noble and Don Pedro does seem to want Claudio's happiness, even if he enjoys his plans for bringing it about.

Annotations (right margin):
- Context and clear focus
- Aware of relationship
- Selecting and highlighting detail
- Apt reference
- Judging
- Speculating, giving alternatives
- Evaluating
- Alternative interpretations
- Speculating about characters
- Language and effects
- Interesting speculation
- Assured conclusion

Examiner comment

Student 2 shows a confident understanding of what is going on in the extract, and backs up the discussion with apt and brief reference to the wider context of the play. Features that mark out this response as of a high quality are the cautious speculations and alternative interpretations of the characters' motivations, as well as the close focus on language. This response would receive a mark representing A*.

Writing about characters' feelings

When writing about the ways in which a character shows his or her feelings in a play, you will need to pay close attention to the words and phrases the character uses, as well as to stage directions.

My Mother Said I Never Should, by Charlotte Keatley, is a play about a family of four generations of women: Doris, her daughter Margaret, her granddaughter Jackie, and her great-granddaughter Rosie. In the extract below Rosie, a teenager, has just found out that Jackie, who she thought was her older sister, is in fact her mother. Jackie gave birth to Rosie as the result of an affair with a married man when she was a student, and had been unable to bring her up as a single parent.

The following activity will help you focus on writing about the feelings a character reveals, and how these feelings are shown to the audience.

Activity 1

Read the extract from the play, and make notes in answer to the question:

Look closely at how Jackie speaks and behaves here. What does it reveal about her feelings?

My Mother Said I Never Should

ROSIE: If you were really my mum you wouldn't have been able to give me away!

JACKIE: How dare you! (*She goes to hit Rosie but cannot*) You're at the centre of everything I do! (*A slight pause*) Mummy treated me as though I'd simply fallen over and cut my knee, – picked me up and said you'll be all right now, it won't show much. She wanted to make it all better. (*Quietly*) … She was the one who wanted it kept secret… I WANTED you, Rosie. (*Angrily*) For the first time in my life I took care of myself – refused joints, did exercises, went to clinic. (*Pause*) 'It's a girl'. (*She smiles irresistibly*) – After you'd gone I tried to lose that memory. (*Pause. With effort*) Graham… your father. (*Silence*) He couldn't be there the day you were born, he had to be in Liverpool. He was married. (*Emphatically*) He loved me, he loved you, you must believe that! (*Pause*) He said he'd leave his wife, but I knew he wouldn't; there were two children, the youngest was only four… we'd agreed, separate lives. I wanted to bring you up. He sent money. (*Pause*) I took you to Lyme Park one day, I saw them together, across the lake, he was buying ice-creams, his wife was taking a photo. I think they live in Leeds now, I saw his name in the Guardian last year, an article about his photographs… (*Pause*) It was a very cold winter after you were born. There were power cuts. I couldn't keep the room warm; there were no lights in the tower blocks; I knew he had an open fire, it was trendy; so we took a bus to Didsbury, big gardens, pine kitchens, made a change from concrete. I rang the bell. (*She stops*) A Punjabi man answered, said he was sorry… they'd moved. By the time we got back to Hulme it was dark, the lift wasn't working – (*She stops*) That was the night I phoned Mummy. (*With difficulty*) Asked her. (*Pause*) I tried! I couldn't do it, Rosie. (*Pause*) It doesn't matter how much you succeed afterwards, if you've failed once. (*Pause*) After you'd gone… I kept waking in the night to feed you… A week… in the flat… Then I went back to art school. Sandra and Hugh thought I was inhuman. I remember the books that came out that winter – how to succeed as a single working mother – fairy-tales! (*Pause*) Sandra and Hugh have a family now. Quite a few of my friends do. (*Pause*) I could give you everything now. Rosie?…

Pause

ROSIE: I used to hate you, only I never knew why. (*She gestures*) Sit down on the swing. I'm going to Oldham, to live with Gran – Great-Gran. Dad says I can.

Jackie hesitates

JACKIE: I'm frightened.

Peer/Self-assessment

When you have written your own response to an extract question on character, compare it with the work of Students 1 and 2 on pages 114–115. You could carry out the steps below on your own work, or swap with a partner, looking at each other's written responses.

- Annotate the response in the same way as the examiner annotated Student 1 and Student 2's responses.
- Now try to grade the answer, using the mark scheme in 'Moving up the grades' on page 137.
- Write down three things that would improve the quality of the response.
- Looking at your own work, decide which skills you have developed and used successfully in this response.
- Which skills do you need to develop further?
- Plan how you will achieve the improvements that have been identified as appropriate to your own work.

GradeStudio

Getting the grade!

Here are two student responses to the task on page 113. Read the answers, together with the examiner's comments. As you read the responses, make particular note of the specific points that are made about the character Jackie's feelings.

B grade answer

Student 1

Focus — In the passage, Jackie seems to differ in the way she behaves and how she — **A bit general**
speaks. Jackie seems to act very defensively after Rosie makes the accusation
that if she was her real mum, Jackie would not have given her away, by replying
angrily, shouting, 'How dare you!' This is an indication of angry emotions — **General**
because of how this can be imagined to be said but also the stage direction
which is given after, when it says 'She goes to hit Rosie but cannot'. Jackie — **Apt reference – but could develop**
Focus on detail – some appreciation of style and effect — then continues in a hasty and angry manner, which is represented when Jackie
claims that 'I WANTED you, Rosie'. In this line Jackie emphasises the word — **Discussing**
'wanted' what she is saying will get through to Rosie. What this reveals about — **Yes – valid**
her feelings is that Jackie is desperate to let Rosie know that she did want to
keep her as her own child, which is also shown when she says 'I wanted to bring
Develops point — you up'. After this she explains and reminisces about the time that Jackie
had to phone up her mum asking if she was able to bring up Rosie as her own. — **Sensible discussion**
She tells this to Rosie with great awkwardness, as is suggested by the painful
memory she is revisiting, and when the stage directions say that this is said
Well noted — 'With difficulty'. Jackie also finds it difficult to get this across to Rosie when
she is adamant that she tried, as is indicated when she admits, 'After you'd — **Discussing J's motives**
gone… I kept waking in the night to feed you… A week… in the flat'. She then
explains to Rosie about how she tried to be a good mum when she recalls 'the
Selects, but doesn't develop — books that came out that winter'. Jackie then seems to reveal all in the last
line when she admits, 'I'm frightened'.

Examiner comment

Student 1 has discussed Jackie's speech and behaviour thoughtfully, and with some sensitivity. Some of the points are not developed as far as they could be, however, and are left hanging (note, for example, the ending to the response, where the point about Jackie being frightened is not explored). This response would earn a mark representing a good B. Building on the strengths here, such as the exploration of stage directions and the sensitive discussion of Jackie's feelings, would have resulted in a higher grade.

Student 2

In the passage, Jackie begins by saying 'How dare you!' This shows us that she is stunned by what Rosie has said and is, possibly, disgusted by it and appalled. The fact that she goes to hit her further highlights this point and suggests that she is quite hurt and angry. However, because she cannot do so we see that she really cares for, and can't bring herself to inflict pain on, Rosie. The fact that she says, 'I WANTED you, Rosie' shows us the frustration she feels and how strongly she wants Rosie to understand the situation and realise that she didn't want to give her up.

Jackie goes on to describe the pregnancy, 'For the first time in my life I took care of myself'. This shows us that she really tried to be responsible and cared about the health of her child. When she smiles 'irresistibly' when she remembers finding out 'It's a girl', it reinforces the fact that she cares for her; she is showing affection towards her baby. When she is talking about Rosie's father, she tells her that 'He loved me, he loved you'. This shows us that she cares for Rosie's emotions and wants to ensure that she doesn't feel abandoned. She reinforces this by saying, 'you must believe that!' She is trying to convince Rosie but it suggests that she is almost trying to convince herself.

When she is talking about the night she had to phone her mum we get the impression that she was ashamed. She says it 'With difficulty', showing she finds it hard to talk about because she thinks what she did was wrong. She tries to justify what she has done by saying, 'I tried! I couldn't do it, Rosie.' She is admitting to Rosie what happened, that she wasn't able to bring up her own child. She is showing her that it was not an easy decision, that she did try but wasn't able to succeed. She ends up saying, 'I could give you everything now', which suggests that she wants to prove that she is worthy of her daughter, she wants to be reunited with her daughter and now feels that she is able to do a good job of this and wants to be forgiven. At the end of the extract, it's as if the roles are reversed, with Rosie telling Jackie to 'Sit down', while Jackie simply says, 'I'm frightened'. Perhaps this suggests that it has suddenly occurred to her that she may now lose Rosie for ever.

Annotations:
- Strong opening, with clear focus
- Stage direction
- Building up points
- Astute and sensitive
- Closely read – good inference
- Thorough discussion
- Close focus on language and effect
- Sensitive evaluation
- Supported inference
- Evaluating
- Sensitive speculation

Examiner comment

Student 2 is focused on the question from the very start, and maintains this focus throughout the response – look at how many specific points are made about Jackie's feelings. This is supported by really close reading of words and phrases, including stage directions, which are key in this extract. This is a sensitive and evaluative response, with clear evidence of analysis and appreciation. Consequently, it would receive a mark representing A*.

MOVING UP THE GRADES

How to go up the grades

Both responses discuss the character's speech and behaviour thoughtfully, but Student 2 has a tighter focus on the question all the way through the response, and has developed the points made in greater detail. Each point made in Student 2's response is explored with insight and sensitivity and is well supported by detail. There are elements of this in Student 1's response, but it is not quite as developed or analytical.

Putting it into practice

Look at the two responses here and note the similarities and differences between them. Write down three reasons why Student 2 gets the better mark, giving specific examples from what they have written to support the points you have noted.

3.2 Drama essay questions

In Unit 2 you will answer one out of a choice of two questions on the drama text you have studied, either contemporary or literary heritage.

The pattern of questions will be similar for all drama texts. The following questions are typical of the questions you are likely to see in your exams.

Higher tier questions

On the Higher tier you will find questions such as:

▶ For which of the characters in the play do you have the most sympathy? Show how the presentation of your chosen character creates sympathy for him or her.
▶ What do you think of … and the way he/she is presented in the play?
▶ Show how … presents the relationship between … and …
▶ Give advice to the actor playing … on how he/she should present the character to an audience.
▶ Imagine you are … At the end of the play, you think back over its events. Remember how … would speak when you write your answer.
▶ How does … present the theme of … in the play?
▶ The play … has been described as '…'. What features of the play may make it have this sort of effect on an audience?
▶ To what extent do you find the title of the play effective?

These are the assessment criteria that you will be assessed against.

Assessment Objectives:

AO1 Respond to texts critically and imaginatively; select and evaluate relevant textual detail to illustrate and support interpretations.

AO2 Explain how language, structure and form contribute to writers' presentation of ideas, themes and settings.

AO4 Relate texts to their social, cultural and historical contexts; explain how texts have been influential and significant to self and other readers in different contexts and at different times.

Foundation tier questions

On the Foundation tier you will find questions such as:

▷ Write about the character in the play for whom you have the most sympathy. Explain why you have the most sympathy for him or her.

▷ What do you think of …? [with bullet points to help you organise your answer]

▷ Write about the relationship between … and … Explain why it changes at different points in the play.

▷ Give advice to the actor playing … on how he/she should speak and behave at different points in the play.

▷ Imagine you are … At the end of the play you think back over its events. Write down your thoughts and feelings.

▷ Write about two or three parts of the play that you think an audience would find funny/sad/dramatic/exciting, etc. Explain why you think your chosen parts would have these effects on an audience.

▷ Why do you think … called his/her play '…'? [with bullet points to help you organise your answer]

Examiner tips

● Questions on the Foundation tier tend to be similar in focus to those on the Higher tier, but will be more simply expressed, and are more likely to have bullet points to guide you.

● If an essay question has bullet points, it's important to use them to provide a framework for your answer – and to write as much as you can on *each* bullet point.

● In the exam you will improve your answer if you focus closely on the question. Students often find it helpful to underline the key points of the question, to make sure that their focus is clear.

My learning objectives ▼

- to develop confidence in responding to drama essay questions by learning how to find my way around a drama text
- to develop confidence in responding to drama essay questions by learning how to write to advise an actor

Finding your way around your drama text

It's all very well knowing the story of your set play, but in the exam you will need to be able to quickly call on the key points you should be referring to in order to address the question.

The following activity will help you establish an overview of your set play.

Activity 1

Working on your own or with a partner, try to summarise the key points of your set drama text in as close to 50 words as possible. Think of the type of summary that might be used in publicity if the play were to be performed in a theatre. Read this summary of *An Inspector Calls* by J.B. Priestley to give you an idea of how this may be achieved:

> A prosperous businessman's family have its complacency shattered by the arrival of a mysterious police inspector. He reveals that each of them was involved with a pregnant working-class woman who has committed suicide. A shocking series of twists at the end suggest punishment awaits those who won't confront their responsibilities.

Now write your own 50-word summary. Try to include an overview of the key events, and references to important themes.

GradeStudio

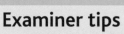

Examiner tips

- In the exam you need to be able to quickly bring to mind key details from your set drama text.
- You need to select and highlight key details to support the points you want to make.
- Examiners are always impressed by someone providing a clear overview of the text.

Plays are built around dramatic moments, or moments of conflict, which may be physical conflict (fights) or mental conflict (arguments). The following activity will help you identify moments of conflict in your set play.

Activity 2

1   Working on your own or in a small group, look over your set play and identify five key dramatic moments, or moments of conflict. You may like to present these in the form of a wall poster.

2   For each moment you have chosen, provide the following details:
- what happens during this part of the play (summed up in a sentence or two)
- what sparks off the conflict
- which characters are involved
- how this moment is important in the play as a whole – the impact it has on future events
- a key quotation to sum up the moment.

In the exam you may be asked to write giving advice to the actor playing one of the main parts in your set play. To make a successful answer, it is useful to imagine that the actor you are giving advice to is not familiar with the play, so you need to explain his or her part in the story. Some students choose to write as if they are actually addressing the actor (using 'you'), while some write in the third person (using 'he' or 'she'). Both approaches are equally valid.

The following activity will help you organise your ideas for this type of question.

Activity 3

1 Working either on your own or in a small group, choose a main character from the play you are studying.

2 Work through this list of questions that an actor unfamiliar with the play may need answered. If you are in a group, you could complete this task as a role-play.
   - In brief, what is the play about?
   - How does my character fit into the play as a whole?
   - When does the audience hear about or see my character for the first time?
   - What first impressions should the audience get of him/her?
   - What are the most important scenes in the play for my character?
   - How are these scenes important in the play as a whole?
   - How does my character interact with other characters?
   - Do my character's relationships with other characters change at all? If so, how and why?
   - What is the most important thing in the world to my character?
   - What quotation from the play best sums up my character?
   - What is the last sight the audience has of my character, and how should the audience react to or feel about this?

3 Now develop your ideas into a response to the following question (fill in the name of your chosen character):

   Give advice to the actor playing … on how he/she should present the character to an audience.

GradeStudio

Examiner tips

In the exam you will improve your answer if you:
- show detailed knowledge of the whole play
- give your ideas of why the character is behaving as he/she does
- avoid giving general advice, such as 'speak loudly'.

Remember, you do **not** need to write about costumes, make-up, lighting or stage effects.

GradeStudio

Check your answers

Look back at your answer.
- Have you selected relevant details from the *whole* of the play?
- Have you discussed how the character relates to other characters?
- Have you explained how the character is important to the play as a whole – perhaps by showing how he or she highlights the play's themes, or has an impact on what happens?

GradeStudio

Getting the grade!

Read the following two student responses to this task on Arthur Miller's play, *A View From The Bridge*:

Give advice to the actor playing Marco on how he should present the character to an audience.

Read the students' answers together with the examiner's comments. As you read, ask yourself how helpful each answer would be to someone who doesn't know much, if anything, about the play.

D grade answer

Student 1

To play Marco you need to be firm. Marco needs to be portrayed as a strong man who doesn't necessarily say a lot, but when he does, it counts, it stands. He needs to be shown as a quiet but dangerous man who is capable. As the actor, you would need to hold a pose; strong, manly, proud; you need to stand upright, with your head held high and a stern face not showing your worries; showing worries is a sign of weakness for Marco as people can play on those emotions.

Some awareness

General discussion, but vague

You need to represent Marco as a man who values family, cares for them. You also need to show him as a man with respect for others; respect for Eddie; don't question or argue with him, take his side in cases. Yet you need to show Marco as someone who stands his ground and follows his beliefs; stand up for your brother Rodolfo, get in Eddie's face when and if Eddie goes against your beliefs and/or you and your brother, talk sternly, quietly and very seriously to Eddie too, it shows the audience 'you mean business' and it shows them Marco can fight back.

Specific detail needed to support

Some general comments on characters and relationships

You also need to, when a conversation is taking place, look away, don't focus on what's being said unless it is directed at you or involves you as this shows respecting privacy. You should talk only when necessary and think about the answer, so take time to answer as it shows the audience you know what you're talking about.

Vague

Examiner comment

Although there is an emerging awareness of the character of Marco here, the response has a weak structure, with no real reference to the events of the play. The references to the way the actor should stand are not sufficient as they are presented here – such comments would only be valid if they were then connected to specific moments in the play, and then to discussion of the character's behaviour. This response would get a mark representing a low grade D. It fails the crucial test, as it would be of very limited use to an actor unfamiliar with the play.

MOVING UP THE GRADES

How to go up the grades

Student 1 does appear to know something of the character's role in the play, and has some strong ideas about him, but these qualities are not clear enough in the response, which is badly lacking in detailed reference to specific events. Student 2 uses specific details from the play to support their sensitive evaluation of the character, and that is why their response would get a much higher mark.

A* **grade answer**

Student 2

Marco is a character whose actions mean more than what he says. At the beginning, Marco should be seen as the sensible one when compared to Rodolfo. When Rodolfo is in awe of America, Marco should still be seen as a character who doesn't get taken up by the American dream, but remembers his duty towards his family; a recurring theme in this play. His love of family should clearly be portrayed. He speaks compassionately about his wife who feeds their kids from 'her own mouth'. As a result when Eddie mentions how when Marco goes back there might be 'a few more mouths to feed' his expression on his face should show how insulted he felt, but it should be hidden by politely commenting on it, such as by saying 'It is not so free there' in a polite manner that does not insult Eddie. He must treat Eddie with utmost respect because of his obligations towards him as Eddie allows Marco and his brother, Rodolfo, to stay with him. As a result, Marco should compassionately, with tears in his eyes, say how grateful he is to Eddie. Therefore, when Eddie says anything, he should fully accept it such as immediately responding to Eddie's request (through jealousy) of wanting Rodolfo to not sing by the excuse of saying 'he might get picked up'. However, when his family, or his code of honour and justice is at risk, he must show his anger, either symbolically or through his response. For example, family is important to him so when he sees Rodolfo being hit, he must show his instant reaction to show to Eddie that he will be there for his family. Therefore, when Marco picks up the chair and lifts it with one hand 'like a weapon', there must be compassion in his actions and facial expressions that portray more than words, so that this scene becomes symbolic. This section must be done in defiance because this is Marco's first attack against Eddie. When something is more important to him, such as justice and codes of honour, he must be vehement in his response. He must immediately be aware that it was Eddie who called the immigration office. This is something which Marco should not be able to take as he comes from the old traditional part of Sicily where you do not betray your family. As a result, he must accuse Eddie with harshness when he exclaims, 'It was that one' in front of the community where Eddie had found his identity. Marco must say this so believably so the community believe Marco as well.

The character playing Marco must fully understand Marco's sense of injustice that the law cannot do anything for the hideous crime that Eddie committed. Therefore, when he says, 'all the law is not in a book', he must say it with such disgust that he spits and turns the knife on Eddie, and it seems justifiable.

Marco is a character in the play who says the least, but his actions show more than words. When he kills Eddie, he must not show any remorse even though he goes against his own code of honour by breaking his promise.

Discussion of characters and relationships

Focused overview

Subtle understanding of character, backed by direct reference

Apt reference to stage directions

Appreciation of context

Astute point about important moment in the play

Sensitive to characters and relationships – reference to structure (could develop still further)

Key reference

Social/historical context

Understands wider implications

Sensitive and evaluative, with confident integration of detail

Well understood

Examiner summary

This response would be extremely useful to an actor unfamiliar with the play. The student uses a sound and detailed knowledge of the text to support their sensitive evaluation of the character. The references to the play's cultural and social context are well handled, whilst sight is never lost of the focus of the question. This answer would get a mark representing A*.

Writing about characters

In the exam the question may be quite open, and you may have to choose a character to write about – it may be the one you have most sympathy for; the one you have least sympathy for; the one you find most, or least, to blame; and so on. You need to show your understanding of your chosen character, and to support your judgements with detailed reference to the events of the play. It will also help if you think about the way your chosen character relates to other characters, the reasons why they may speak and behave as they do and how they may reflect the important themes in the play.

The following activity will help you sort out your thoughts about a character from your drama text.

Activity 1

1 Working either on your own or in a small group, choose a main character from the play you are studying.

2 On a large sheet of paper, draw a figure in the centre to represent your chosen character (stick figures are fine!).

3 Around the drawing of the character, add the following (if you are working in a group, discuss and agree your ideas first):
- An animal, bird or insect that best represents your chosen character. Explain your choice.
- A plant, tree or flower that best represents your chosen character. Explain your choice.
- A symbol to represent your chosen character.
- The key motivation of your chosen character – the single thing that is most important in his or her life.
- One quotation to sum up your chosen character.

4 Present and explain your ideas to the rest of the class.

Here is an example of an answer to Activity 1. This answer uses the character of Catherine in A View from the Bridge but this is only a suggestion. There are many other, equally valid ideas, for this character and for other characters – the important thing is that you have a good reason for every point you make.

represents Rodolfo's words to Catherine "If I take in my hands a little bird. And she grows and wishes to fly..."

key motivation – life with Rodolfo

key quotation – "Eddie, I never meant to do nothing bad to you."

symbolises her vulnerability and hidden strength

represents Eddie's words to Catherine "What's the high heels for, Garbo?"

In the exam you may be asked to imagine you are a character from the play. You may be asked to tell the story of the play, or important parts of it, from the character's point of view.

The following activity will show how the same events may be interpreted in different ways, depending on the point of view of the person relating them. It will also give you practice in selecting and highlighting relevant details.

Activity 2

1 Choose a key scene from the play you are studying.
2 Identify the two or three most important characters in your chosen scene.
3 Make notes on your chosen characters' thoughts and feelings during the scene. Think about how the scene fits into the whole story, the important points in the scene, how other characters behave, and, perhaps, which themes are highlighted in your chosen scene.
4 Write a few paragraphs from the point of view of each of your chosen characters.

GradeStudio
Check your answers

Look back on your answer.
● Have you selected relevant details from the chosen scene?
● Have you included references to themes, other characters/relationships, and the rest of the play?
● Have you managed to sound like the character/s? (You can test this, by asking someone else if they can tell who it is!)

Look at the following openings to responses on *Othello*, by William Shakespeare. The play tells the story of a black army general, Othello, who at the beginning of the play has eloped with Desdemona, a much younger white woman. She is the daughter of Brabantio, an important man in Venice, where the play begins.

Iago is a fellow soldier of a lower rank who bears a grudge against Othello, possibly because Othello has promoted Cassio rather than him. Iago stops at nothing to gain his revenge. His plottings eventually result in the deaths of his own wife, Emilia; of Roderigo, a foolish Venetian whom he uses ruthlessly; of Desdemona; and of Othello himself.

The students are responding to the following question:

For which of Iago's victims do you have the most sympathy, and why?

As you read the openings to their responses, rate their focus on the question.

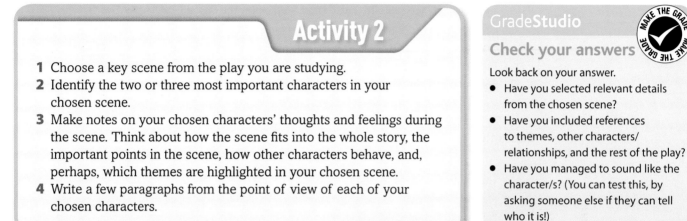

Example 1

I have sympathy for all Iago's victims as he deeply hurts and destroys them all. Cassio loses his job, which he probably earned and deserved. Desdemona is accused of betraying Othello, and Roderigo is killed by Iago. I feel extremely sorry for Emilia as she is forced to help her 'wayward' husband out of duty and respect. Iago however does not appreciate her and constantly insults her: 'It is a common thing'.

The victim of Iago's devilish plots I feel most sorry for, though, is Othello. First this is because of the way he speaks of Othello behind his back. He stirs prejudice from Brabantio against Othello by telling him 'an old black ram is tupping your white ewe'. This crude animal imagery is not relevant to Othello and I feel sorry for him as Iago is presenting him in this way.

Example 2

The character I have the most sympathy for is Othello. Through the course of this play Iago manages to undermine and trick Othello to the point of destruction when he turns into the 'green-eyed monster'. Othello truly is Iago's number one victim. Othello is such a respected, noble gentleman among the Venetians, but because he's black, Iago manages to use this as a flaw. He sees Othello as impure even though Othello, the experienced general, has started from the bottom and earned his status and respect. We feel sympathy for Othello at the beginning because he is unaware that Iago, his supposedly loyal servant, is saying bad things about Othello behind his back.

Example 3

Out of all of Iago's victims, I feel most sympathy for Othello because he does not deserve to have his mind poisoned by Iago. Othello has a nice life planned ready for him but it ends in tragedy. He has Desdemona, a woman he opened his heart to and fell in love with, to which she did the same, and they are married, he has a job he loves, he travels the world and has great friends, but all of that ends. I believe that Iago ruins Othello's life because he is jealous (the theme of this play is jealousy). I believe Iago does not intend for things to go as far as they do because towards the end he tries to make Othello think Desdemona is innocent although Cassio is guilty.

GradeStudio

How to go up the grades

The first two examples show different, equally valid, approaches. Example 1 is well focused in the first sentence, then discusses Iago's relationships with other characters, before closing in on the main focus of the response. Example 2, on the other hand, focuses on the chosen character (Othello, again) from the start, and immediately supports the judgement by evaluating Iago's behaviour. Example 3 starts quite well, with a good focus on the question, but then loses some focus and tends to lack clarity.

The following activity will help you write an effective opening for your essay.

Activity 3

1   Choose one of the following questions to work on.

Either

For which character do you have the most sympathy? Give reasons for your choice and support your answer with detailed reference to the text.

Or

For which character do you have the least sympathy? Give reasons for your choice and support your answer with detailed reference to the text.

2   Decide on the character you will write about, and think of good reasons for your choice.
3   Make notes about:
   • why you've chosen the character
   • the first time the audience sees or hears about your character, and how that may affect the audience's (or your) feelings towards him or her
   • important scenes throughout the play for your chosen character
   • the relationships your character has with other characters, and how this affects your or an audience's feelings towards him or her
   • the last time the audience see, or hear of, your chosen character, and the effects of this
   • a final summing up of your feelings about the character.

4   Now write the first paragraph to your response.
5   Swap your opening paragraph with that of a partner. Look at your partner's answer and decide on the following.
   • Has he or she made a good start by giving a clear opinion from the beginning?
   • Is there a clear overview of the character's role in the play?
   • Is a close knowledge of the play shown right from the start?
   • Have points been linked back to the question?

6   Discuss with your partner the strengths of your work and the areas for improvement in your responses.

The following activity will help you maintain focus throughout your essay.

Activity 4

1   Following on from the introduction you wrote in Activity 3, write another section (a paragraph or two) of the same essay, using the notes you made earlier.

2   When you have written this, swap your work with a partner. Check your partner's answer.
   • Does it make clear reference to the question?
   • Does it make relevant reference to the text?
   • Does it avoid simple story telling?
   • Does it maintain focus on the question?

GradeStudio

Examiner tips

• It makes a real difference to have a strong opening to your response.
• You should aim to refer to the question right from the start.
• If you can link your choice of character to his or her role in the play as a whole, you will be giving an overview, which is a skill associated with the higher grades.
• Remember, in the exam you will have 40 minutes to answer the essay question.

Read the further extracts below from the essays on *Othello* (the openings of the essays are on page 124). As a reminder, the question is:

For which of Iago's victims do you have the most sympathy, and why?

As you read, check the focus of the responses. Try making a note of each time there is specific reference to the question, and of each time a point made is supported by reference to the text. Once you have read all three extracts, try putting them in rank order, from the one with the tightest focus, to the one with the least.

Example 1

Othello tells us how much he loves Desdemona by saying at the beginning of the play he could die happy. The way Iago takes this away from him is heart wrenching. I pity Othello as through Iago he has lost the most important person in the world to him. Iago seems to pour himself into Othello throughout the play, causing Othello to curse more, and doubt his wife. I feel sorry for Othello towards the end of the play as he seems to descend into madness, as a result of believing Iago's lies. His speech becomes disjointed and increasingly violent.

Example 2

We feel sympathy for Othello at the beginning because he is unaware that Iago, his supposedly loyal servant, is saying bad things about Othello behind his back. He bluntly describes Othello and Desdemona to her father Brabantio, saying that a 'black ram is tupping your white ewe', which leads to carnage in the end because Desdemona, loyal Desdemona decides to support her husband instead of her father. Othello is clearly just unaware and that is why we sympathise with him. He is unaware Iago is planting the seeds of jealousy in his mind, that he's taking pay from Roderigo to cause awkwardness and havoc, he's unaware that Iago planted the sentimental handkerchief in Cassio's belongings and he's unaware that all this destruction will inevitably lead to him killing his loyal wife Desdemona. Innocent Othello gains even more sympathy because he does not doubt Iago throughout the play – not once does he question Iago.

Example 3

I believe that Iago ruins Othello's life because he is jealous (the theme of this play is jealousy). I believe Iago does not intend for things to go as far as they do because towards the end he tries to make Othello think Desdemona is innocent although Cassio is guilty. Yet Othello's mind is too poisoned already and he believes she has given Cassio the handkerchief and is having an affair even though she is innocent. I also believe that death is too harsh a punishment for Desdemona and that Othello has started to go crazy by the end thanks to Iago. I assume that Iago only wants Othello to kill or demote Cassio and promote Iago as lieutenant, not go crazy and kill people.

GradeStudio

How to go up the grades

An examiner would rank these extracts in the following order: Example 2, then Example 1, and finally, Example 3.

Example 1 shows empathy for Othello, and focuses on the question, but tends to rush through the points made. This answer would be improved by discussing the points made and providing evidence for them with closer reference to the detail of the play. Example 2 has a really clear focus throughout – look at the way the words 'sympathy' and 'sympathise' keep cropping up. Also notice the use of specific details from the play. Example 3 shows real enthusiasm, but this student has fallen into the trap of letting enthusiasm get in the way of answering the question, and forgetting to focus clearly on it in the anxiety to show off his or her knowledge of the play.

Putting it into practice

Check your own responses to ensure that you:
- use the words of the question throughout your response
- avoid just telling the story.

The following activity will help you write a well-focused conclusion.

Activity 5

1   Continuing with the essay you have been writing sample paragraphs for in Activities 3 and 4, write a concluding paragraph.
2   When you have completed your concluding paragraph, swap your work with a partner. Check your partner's answer.
   • Has the paragraph pulled together all the ideas in the essay?
   • Is there clear reference to the question?

Read the concluding paragraphs to the essays on *Othello* that were discussed on pages 124–127. Judge to what extent these students have summed up their ideas, and ended strongly.

Example 1

> And so Othello is the character I feel most sympathy for because after all he's done, after all the battles he's won in order to emerge victorious, gain respect and status, despite his racial background, he has been taken advantage of by Iago because of a petty promotion. Iago, knowing full well of Othello's pride and trust, takes advantage of it, and uses it to sow the seeds of jealousy and cause him to end his life by becoming the 'green-eyed monster' and killing Desdemona.

Example 2

> So I believe that he kills himself to be with Desdemona in the afterlife after he learns the truth at the end of the play, so that is why I feel most sympathy for Othello.

Example 3

> I sympathise with Othello as he seems to lose himself, consumed by Iago's clever lies and evil. Finally he murders the woman he loves, though instead of feeling anger towards him, it causes me to pity him even more. He has been cruelly tricked into killing the love of his life, and when he realises this tragedy could have been prevented is when my sympathy for him reaches its peak. He has by far suffered the most at the hands of the villain Iago.

GradeStudio

Examiner tips

In the exam you will improve your answers if you:

● use specific details to show you know the text well
● discuss the behaviour of the other characters thoughtfully and sensitively
● refer to key themes.

Foundation Tier candidates may be asked to focus on specific parts of the text.

Higher Tier candidates will be expected to show knowledge of the whole text.

GradeStudio

How to go up the grades

All three conclusions make clear reference to the question about which of Iago's victims the student feels most sympathy for. The conclusion of Example 1 is thoughtful and evaluative right to the end, and makes good use of knowledge of the text. The final paragraph of Example 3 is also well focused, and clear in its point of view, although is not quite as assured as that of Example 1. The conclusion in Example 2 is focused, but brief and under-developed, and is the least successful of the three.

Putting it into practice

Now judge your own concluding paragraph, written in Activity 5.
How would you rate your paragraph, comparing it with the levels of response in the three examples?

GradeStudio

Getting the grade!

Read the following two student responses, together with the examiner's comments. The responses are based on *Blood Brothers* by Willy Russell, which tells the story of twins separated shortly after birth. Linda is a central character, who has known the twins – Mickey Johnstone and Edward Lyons – for most of their lives.

The students are writing in response to this question:

Imagine you are Linda. At the end of the play you think back over its events. Write down your thoughts and feelings. Remember how Linda would speak when you write your answer.

D grade answer

Student 1

How could this happen! Is it all my fault? If only I had loved Mickey the way I should have… none of this would have happened. I loved Mickey… but I also loved Eddie. Brothers! I can't believe it, they couldn't believe it, and now it's all ruined. We were all best of friends once. That was a long time ago though. Before Edward went to university. And before Mickey went on those bloody drugs!… If only we could go back, back to playing and singing in the streets… back to the good old times.

> Aware of characters and relationships

> References to some events in the text

Listen to me, all sad 'cos I lost two lovers… two friends. What about poor Mrs J, what a lovely lady, how did she deserve this. It would have been bad enough just losing her Mickey, but she lost her Eddie too. I don't understand what happened, but it wasn't her fault, poor woman.

> Aware of characters and relationships

> Reference to character – but does this sound like Linda?

That Mrs Lyons, she's a nasty bitch, it's her fault!… Hers or mine. If she had kept her mouth shut, neither of them would be dead, but if I'd never have cheated, it wouldn't have happened. She tried to keep them away. Tried to help Eddie… to help Mickey. She even moved away. What did I do to help? Nothing, nothing!

> Empathy and awareness

> Reference to text

They woulda been alrigh' if it weren't for me. They would still be laughin' 'bout things an' joking around… Goodbye Mickey, I love you. Goodbye Eddie, I love you too… I'm so sorry, boys.

> Empathy

Examiner comment

This answer shows a clear awareness of Linda's possible thoughts and feelings and, mostly, sounds like Linda. With more references to key events in the text, this could have been a grade C but as it stands, it would get a mark representing a grade D.

MOVING UP THE GRADES

How to go up the grades

Student 1 only makes a few general references to key events in the text, these could have been developed further to achieve a better grade. To get further to A*, Student 2 needed to make more specific reference to Linda's reactions to the key events at the end of the play.

Putting it into practice

Look at the two student responses and make a list of the similarities and differences between them. Then write down three things that made Student 2 get the better mark.

Student 2

My *God*, I can't believe it, I just can't. My Mickey, mine. I loved him so much, no matter how much I told him it never got old. And Eddie, my love grew for him more and more as the days got on. He had done so much for us, he would have done anything for me and Mickey. •———————————————————————— | Strong sense of character and relationships |

We had known each other since we were kids. I've got so many memories of us three, playing cowboys, cops and robbers. I wouldn't change a day I spent with Mickey and Eddie. Not even the time Mickey found Sammy's air rifle and we all ended up getting told off by the police because Eddie didn't know when to keep his mouth shut.• | References to key events |

It seemed like a dream come true when we all found each other in the countryside again. All the fun started all over again. Of course by then I knew my feeling towards Mickey, I told him every day, before school, 'Mickey, I love you' and after school, 'Mickey I love you'. He was too shy though, it only used to embarrass him. I don't know if we would ever have got together if it wasn't for Eddie. Eddie had such a good heart, he told me that he loved me and the same day he told Mickey to get his act together. Eddie just wanted to make me happy, that's who he was, he would've done anything to please you.• | Sensitive references to characters and relationships | Character | Eddie's character and impact on events |

'Course he went off to university, he came from a different class to us and I guess when he went it was the first time me and Mickey ever realised we were different from him. Everything seemed to go downhill from then on really. Mickey lost his job and I conveniently joined the club, mind you Mrs Johnstone was wonderful about it. She let us live at hers, 'until you get yourselves on your feet', she said.• | Reference to theme | Characters and relationships, and good voice |

But then our Sammy led Mickey astray. Mickey's always looked up to Sammy, and to say the least he is not the best role model. Anyway, Mickey ended up doin' time. Seven years they gave him. He got out early for good behaviour, but by then it was too late, it seemed Mickey's personality had drained away. •——— | Characters and relationships | Detail | Sensitive |

I knew exactly what it was: those pills. I hated him taking them but he thought he needed them. One day he even told me 'I take them because they make me invisible'.• | Direct reference |

As you can see, it was a rough time and so for once 'I wondered what the price would be to let the young girl out', and have a bit of fun. Eddie had been helping us a lot. Recently he got Mickey his job and us a house. Not to Mickey's knowledge, mind, he is far too stubborn to ever ask for help. Anyway I grew fonder and fonder of Eddie and, well, we kissed. It was just a kiss between friends, nothing more and nothing less. But even that thought will not comfort me or help me sleep at night. •——— | Detail neatly included | Reference | Character | Sensitive representation of character |

| Reference |

Examiner comment

This is a sensitive and convincing interpretation of Linda's character, showing secure and detailed knowledge of the play, and an ability to evaluate characters and relationships. This answer is worth a high grade A.

Writing about themes in a drama text

Questions on themes may be straightforward to recognise, such as:

- How does … present the theme of … in the play?

However, questions such as the following will also provide opportunities for you to show your knowledge and understanding of the themes of the play:

- How effective do you find the title …?
- Why do you think … decided to call the play …?

The following activity will help you identify the key themes in your set play.

GradeStudio

Examiner tips

- The themes of a play are the main messages the playwright wants the audience to think about.
- It's common to find similar themes in a range of literature – such as conflict between the generations, ambition, jealousy, and so on.

Activity 1

1. Working on your own, or in a group, write the title of your play in the centre of a large sheet of paper.
2. Surrounding the title, and leaving plenty of space around each, write down all the themes you can identify in your set play.
3. You may decide to divide the next tasks between members of your group. For each theme you have identified, make a note of:
   - parts of the play where it features significantly (make sure you cover the whole of the play)
   - characters who exemplify the theme, and a brief explanation of why
   - one or two quotations (the shorter the better) to illustrate the theme.
4. Share your findings with the rest of the class.

The following activity will help you focus on how to write about the themes in your set play.

GradeStudio

Examiner tips

In the exam you will improve your answer if you:

- set out with a clear idea of what you want to say
- always pin down points you make with specific reference to the events of the play
- cover key points from *throughout* the text.

Activity 2

1. Choose one of the following questions and adapt it to your set play:
   - What do you think is the most important theme in …? Show how … presents this theme to an audience.
   - Why do you think … chose to call his/her play …?
   - To what extent do you find … a suitable title for the play?
2. Using the ideas you formulated in Activity 1, make notes on how you could respond to the question. You need to:
   - write a strong introduction, with a clear focus on the question
   - select important parts of the play, from the beginning, middle and end, as well as key parts in between, that illustrate the points you want to make
   - give a thoughtful discussion of characters and relationships
   - focus on how the play is written – this may include dramatic irony (where the audience knows more than the characters), foreshadowing (where what may be an apparently small detail anticipates what will happen later on), the building of dramatic tension, the way people speak and behave, and so on
   - write a strong conclusion, making your overall viewpoint clear.
3. Using the notes you have just made, write the introduction (no more than two paragraphs) to an essay answering the question you have created.

Below are extracts from three responses to questions involving discussion of themes. As you read them, check to what extent they:

- are well organised – each paragraph should stand alone as a sort of mini-essay, with a clear purpose

- make specific reference to events in the play.

The first example is from an essay about *A Taste of Honey*. This play by Shelagh Delaney is set in Salford in the late 1950s, and tells the story of teenager, Jo, and her mother, Helen. When Helen leaves Jo alone, Jo invites a sailor she has just met to stay with her over Christmas. After he has returned to sea, she discovers she is pregnant. Befriended by Geoff, who is gay, and who moves in with her and takes care of her, Jo is happier than she has been for a while – until Helen returns and everything goes wrong. At the end of the play, as Jo goes into labour, she is alone again.

The student is writing in response to the following question:

Why do you think Shelagh Delaney called her play *A Taste of Honey*? To what extent do you find it an effective title?

Example 1

'A Taste of Honey' is an appropriate name for the play because it's quite ironic. For example, the overall mood of the play is actually quite depressing and it doesn't really have a good or happy ending.

This is ironic given the title because 'a taste of honey' implies something sweet or delightful, indicating to the reader that the play is going to be a happy story or have a pleasant ending. This could also be an appropriate title, as the story's main theme is about Jo's hope of a happy life being crushed. This is just like the title being able to make the audience expect a happy ending but then being surprised by the actual depressing story line.

Also 'A Taste of Honey' could be appropriate to the play because it links in with the story. For example, in the play Jo starts off quite happy with finding the man she loves only for him to leave her pregnant to go back to the navy. This is similar to 'a taste of honey' owing to 'taste' implying a little experience of something good. This is like the play's story, as she does have a bit of happiness until it disappears. Also, a taste of honey sounds almost like a question, and may imply doubt in happiness, which is just like Jo's feelings at the end of the play.

The second example is from an essay on *The History Boys* by Alan Bennett. *The History Boys* is set in a boys' grammar school in Sheffield in the 1980s, and follows a group of sixth-form students who are preparing for Oxbridge entrance exams. They are being taught by three teachers with very different teaching styles.

The student is writing in response to the question:

How does Alan Bennett present education in *The History Boys*?

Example 2

Alan Bennett portrays education in many different ways in 'The History Boys'. He firstly portrays it as perhaps a power struggle between the teachers and students. He shows the headmaster wants the boys to attend Oxford out of selfishness, making the school's achievements and grades look more commendable than they have been previously. The boys, however, as much as they want to go, give the impression that however much the teachers want this, they are not overly sure. This implies that although things are friendly on the surface there seems to be a certain amount of hostility between the teachers and the boys. Mrs Lintott mentions to Irwin in a conversation that 'at least you get their problems. I seldom do', suggesting that trust and respect is lacking between some of the students and teachers, reinforcing this trend of distrust and hostility.

The third example is from an essay about Charlotte Keatley's play *My Mother Said I Never Should*. This deals with relationships between mothers and daughters, shown through the four generations of women in a family: Doris, Margaret, Jackie and Rosie, whose lives, and the choices they make, are set against the social changes of the 20th century. The student is writing in response to the question:

How does Charlotte Keatley show changes in women's lives during the 20th century in *My Mother Said I Never Should*?

Example 3

> The 20th century saw a lot of changes in the lives of women. In the early 1900s women didn't even have the vote, but that started to change, partly as a result of the suffragette movement, and then the two World Wars, where women were needed to work in factories and so on, as the men were called away to war. This was followed by the influence of the women's movement in the sixties and seventies, and scientific developments such as with contraception. I think that all these changes had a big impact on women's lives. At the start of the century women were not expected to work and were definitely considered inferior to men, and women were generally expected to get married, but gradually attitudes changed. Charlotte Keatley shows some of these changes in 'My Mother Said I Never Should'.

GradeStudio

How to go up the grades

These three openings to responses on theme-based questions show different approaches. The opening of Example 1 does address the question, which is about the effectiveness of the title, but is not very clearly organised, so the points made, though valid, are all a bit muddled. Example 2 makes clear reference to the question from the start, and then moves on to discuss the different attitudes of the characters in the play. This is the most effective opening of these three. The final example makes a common error: writing about the historical and social context of the play without showing any detailed knowledge of the play itself.

Putting it into practice

Now look again at your introduction to an essay about the themes in your set play. How does it compare to these three openings? If necessary (if it doesn't have the same sort of qualities as Example 2), try re-drafting or rewriting it. You may then choose to develop the introduction into a full response, using the notes you made in Activity 2.

Peer/Self-assessment

Now look at your written response to an essay question on themes in your set play. How does it compare with the three examples above?
You could carry out the steps below on your own work, or swap with a partner, looking at each other's written responses.
- Annotate the response in the same way as the examiner annotated the students' responses to a character-based question on pages 130–131.

- Now try to grade the answer, using the mark scheme in 'Moving up the grades' on page 137.
- Write down three things that would improve the quality of the response.
- Looking at your own work, decide which skills you have developed and used successfully in this response.
- Which skills do you need to develop further?
- Plan how you will achieve the improvements that have been identified as appropriate to your own work.

How ready are you for your English literature exams?

Read the following statements and decide if you feel confident (Green), need a bit more help (Amber), or need to do more work (Red).

	R	A	G
• I have read my set texts several times.			
• I know the stories of my set texts.			
• I know the key events of my set texts.			
• I know what the main themes are in my set texts, and where they are particularly highlighted.			
• I know the stories of the main characters in my set texts, and understand the way they speak and behave at different points in the text.			
• When I focus on specific parts of my set texts, I can select and highlight words and phrases, and show how they are effective.			
• When I answer extract questions, I can focus on the question right from the start, and select and highlight details from the extract to support the points I am making.			
• In my responses to extract questions, I can briefly explain how the extract fits into the text as a whole.			
• In my essay responses, I know how to write a strong introduction, which clearly refers to the question and provides an overview (my 'take' on the question).			
• I can refer to the question asked all the way through my essay responses, making the focus clear throughout.			
• I can express my ideas clearly.			
• I am confident in explaining my ideas about poems I have not previously studied.			
• I am confident about working out the meaning of poems, by starting from the most obvious reading.			
• I know how to focus on words and phrases in poems, and to show how they fit into my interpretations.			
• I know how to discuss similarities and differences between poems.			
• I know how to organise my time efficiently.			

If you can't answer 'yes' confidently to any of these points, now is your chance to put it right before the exams! You will find help on everything in the above list in this book.

What the examiners are looking for at each grade

Peer/Self-assessment

⬆ Moving up the grades

A* Doing all the things required for an A grade consistently and well, with real confidence and succinctness. In Unit 1, assured exploration of similarities and differences between poems.

A Analysis of how the text is written – unpicking the text to show how it works. Giving an evaluation and providing an overview, and showing sensitivity. In Unit 1, exploration of similarities and differences between poems.

B Really thorough and thoughtful discussion, with points well supported by evidence. In Unit 1, discussion of similarities and differences between poems.

C Detailed reference to the text, selecting and highlighting detail in a thorough, systematic and purposeful way. In Unit 1, sensible points about similarities and differences between poems.

D Some references to the text, with some discussion and awareness of characters, themes, mood and atmosphere, and subtext (reading between the lines). In Unit 1, some comparison and contrasting of poems.

E A focus on the question, with some selection of key parts of the text, but not very developed. In Unit 1, straightforward points of comparison between poems.

F General comments, with no real detail. In Unit 1, simple points of comparison between poems.

G A very short response, or with a lot of material just copied out, and major parts missing or wrong. In Unit 1, a brief and simple comparison between poems.

5 Controlled assessment guide

What is controlled assessment?

Your GCSE exam is made up of three parts:

▶ External assessment – the exam for Unit 1

▶ External assessment – the exam for Unit 2

▶ Controlled assessment – where your teacher will give you details of your tasks for Unit 3.

For your written controlled assessment, you will be given your assignment in advance and your teacher will provide guidance. Your assignment will involve linking a play by Shakespeare to poems in the WJEC GCSE Poetry Collection. You will have an opportunity to study for the assignment and prepare your answer. Your teacher will tell you how much time you have to prepare in advance of the actual assessment.

When you write your final version, you will be in 'controlled conditions'. This means there will be a time limit. You will have a clean copy of the WJEC Poetry Collection and the Shakespeare text, and you will be allowed to take one A4 sheet of notes with you into the assessment session. But at this stage, your teacher will not be able to help you.

▶ Make sure that you prepare carefully for the final assessment.

▶ Once you have finished your work you will not be able to change it, so you must take great care to do your best.

What is it worth?

Your controlled assessment is worth 25 per cent of your marks, so it is important that you do well if you want to get a good grade.

What does controlled assessment for GCSE English Literature look like?

Unit 3: poetry and drama (literary heritage)

What is it worth? Unit 3 is worth 25 per cent of your marks.

You will need to write:

- an essay that makes links between a Shakespeare play and poetry drawn from a range chosen from the WJEC GCSE Poetry Collection. You will have four hours to complete this work.

What is assessed?

You will be assessed against the following assessment criteria:

- Respond to texts critically and imaginatively; select and evaluate relevant textual detail to illustrate and support interpretations.
- Explain how language, structure and form contribute to writers' presentation of ideas, themes and settings.

- Make comparisons and explain links between texts, evaluating writers' different ways of expressing meaning and achieving effects.

Your task will involve linking your Shakespeare text to the poetry through theme.

Your task will have three parts:

- writing about the chosen theme in relation to the Shakespeare play
- writing about the chosen theme in relation to some of the poems you have studied
- making links between the way Shakespeare looks at the theme and the way the poets look at the theme.

You will have time to prepare your answer before writing the controlled assessment. Make sure you plan your preparation carefully.

When you are writing the controlled assessment, leave time to check your work carefully, because you will not be allowed to change it after the session.